FORTRESS • 76

SARACEN STRONGHOLDS AD 630–1050

The Middle East and Central Asia

DAVID NICOLLE   ILLUSTRATED BY ADAM HOOK

Series editors Marcus Cowper and Nikolai Bogdanovic

First published in Great Britain in 2008 by Osprey Publishing,
Midland House, West Way, Botley, Oxford OX2 0PH, United Kingdom
443 Park Avenue South, New York, NY 10016, USA
Email: info@ospreypublishing.com

ISBN 978 184603 115 1

Editorial by Ilios Publishing, Oxford, UK (www.iliospublishing.com)
Page layout by Ken Vail Graphic Design, Cambridge, UK (kvgd.com)
Typeset in Sabon and Myriad Pro
Cartography by The Map Studio, Romsey, UK
Index by Alan Thatcher
Originated by PPS Grasmere Ltd, Leeds, UK
Printed in China through Bookbuilders

08 09 10 11 12   10 9 8 7 6 5 4 3 2 1

A CIP catalogue record for this book is available from the British Library.

FOR A CATALOGUE OF ALL BOOKS PUBLISHED BY OSPREY MILITARY
AND AVIATION PLEASE CONTACT:

NORTH AMERICA
Osprey Direct, c/o Random House Distribution Center, 400 Hahn Road,
Westminster, MD 21157
Email: info@ospreydirect.com

ALL OTHER REGIONS
Osprey Direct UK, PO Box 140, Wellingborough,
Northants, NN8 2FA, UK
Email: info@ospreydirect.co.uk

www.ospreypublishing.com

DEDICATION

For Nadima Kremid and her team at the Institut Français du Proche Orient,
Damascus.

ARTIST'S NOTE

Readers may care to note that the original paintings from which the
colour plates in this book were prepared are available for private sale.
All reproduction copyright whatsoever is retained by the Publishers.
All enquiries should be addressed to:

Scorpio Gallery, PO Box 475, Hailsham, East Sussex BN27 2SL, UK

The Publishers regret that they can enter into no correspondence upon
this matter.

THE FORTRESS STUDY GROUP (FSG)

The object of the FSG is to advance the education of the public in the
study of all aspects of fortifications and their armaments, especially
works constructed to mount or resist artillery. The FSG holds an annual
conference in September over a long weekend with visits and evening
lectures, an annual tour abroad lasting about eight days, and an annual
Members' Day.

The FSG journal *FORT* is published annually, and its newsletter *Casemate*
is published three times a year. Membership is international. For further
details, please contact:

The Secretary, c/o 6 Lanark Place, London W9 1BS, UK

Website: www.fsgfort.com

THE WOODLAND TRUST

Osprey Publishing are supporting the Woodland Trust, the UK's leading
woodland conservation charity, by funding the dedication of trees.

CONTENTS

SARACEN STRONGHOLDS
AD 630–1050

Khirbat al-Bayda is a classic example of a Roman-style fortress in the desert frontier zones of what are now Syria and Jordan, which is not Roman but was built for pre-Islamic Ghassanid Arab *phylarchs* or autonomous rulers. (De Boysson photograph)

INTRODUCTION

The historical context

Islamic military architecture had numerous roots. However, there has been a tendency for Western scholars to assume that these were all found outside the Arabian peninsula, and that the first Arab conquerors brought nothing of architectural significance from their supposedly primitive homeland.

In reality the pre-Islamic Arabs did not live only in the Arabian peninsula. Not only were entire tribes and Arabic-speaking towns found deep inside the Graeco-Roman and Iranian empires, but large frontier zones were often governed, either partially or wholly, by Arab vassal dynasties. At the same time the 'superpowers' of Rome-Byzantium and Sassanian Iran dominated large parts of the Arabian peninsula, even including Yemen in the far south.

Though there were towns throughout much of Arabia, these were few, scattered and generally small except in Yemen. However, given the Arab peoples' long involvement in the affairs of neighbouring empires, it is not surprising to find sophisticated Mediterranean and Iranian styles of architecture deep within Arabia. Some examples reflected strong links between Syrian Palmyra and central Arabia, between Jordanian Petra and western Arabia, and between the Kingdom of Hatra in northern Iraq with many parts of Arabia. In the latter case, much of Hatra's army was Arab, and it seems inconceivable that these warriors did not take knowledge of fortification back to their own tribes.

Meanwhile, in pre-Islamic Yemen and some neighbouring areas of southern Arabia, a distinctive indigenous Arabian style of architecture had developed over hundreds, perhaps thousands, of years. Though the pre-Islamic civilization of Yemen had features in common with those of the Fertile Crescent and other regions outside Arabia, it was highly distinctive and very different from the widespread image of pre-Islamic Arabia as a land of warring, nomadic tribes. Based upon irrigation in valleys whose seasonal streams flowed into the desert rather than the sea, it was characterized by occasionally fortified towns. In contrast, the people of western Yemen were more nomadic and had strong cultural links with the other side of the Red Sea in what are now Eritrea and Ethiopia. Here the kingdom of Axum had its own distinctive but little-known architectural tradition, and was seen by the fellow-Christian Byzantine Empire as a rising power in the southern Red Sea area.

The settled, urban areas of what is now Yemen were under local *qayls*, who were royal vassals of the kingdoms into which this part of Arabia was divided. The highlands were similarly under local *qayls*. Militias seem to have been drawn from urban middle classes, though there were also inscriptions referring to *q-r-n* (vowels unknown) 'garrison troops', which might suggest there were fortifications to defend. Other inscriptions describe warfare concentrating upon the taking and holding of towns while defenders tended to withdraw into 'citadels'.

Fortifications also played a significant role in the career of Dhu Nuwas, who founded a ruling dynasty during the first half of the 6th century AD that featured prominently in pre-Islamic Arabic poetry as well as early Arab–Islamic histories. Some of the fortifications mentioned in the history of Dhu Nuwas and the Ethiopian invasion that his activities prompted clearly served as strongpoints where military equipment could be stored in safety. They could also be under the authority of women. Many of these events were located in northern Hijaz, where one such fortified place was Taima, a strategic outpost associated with powerful Jewish tribes and merchants, including weapons merchants who had close links with both Syria and Iran.

The descendants of a small Sassanian army that conquered Yemen were still there when the current Sassanian governor, Badham, came to terms with the Prophet Muhammad. Having converted to Islam, his troops became perhaps the first non-Arab professional troops in the Islamic army, bringing with them Sassanian Iran's sophisticated heritage of siege warfare and fortification. At least as important, however, was an Iranian military influence upon central Arabia via the pro-Sassanian, Arab vassal-state of Hira in Iraq. In contrast Byzantine influence tended to be cultural and economic rather than directly military.

The ruins of the pre-Islamic Christian Arab town of Umm al-Jimal, on the edge of the desert in northern Jordan, date from the 4th to the early 7th centuries AD, and include advanced defensive features such as the box machicolation high above the entrance to this early 5th-century tower. (Author's photograph)

The histories of most of those peoples and states that would be conquered by Islamic armies are better documented. However, the story of their military architecture is not always as clear cut, and was certainly not a story of straightforward technological and architectural 'progress'. While there is compelling evidence that Romano-Byzantine military architecture had a profound influence upon that of the early Islamic period, it was not alone. It also tended to be localized and was much more important during the Umayyad Caliphate (AD 661–750) than in later centuries.

During the pre-Islamic period the frontier zone, or *limes*, between Romano-Byzantine-ruled Syria-Jordan and the Arabian steppes or deserts included strongly fortified towns that mainly served as trading centres. By the 5th and 6th centuries they were similarly dotted with monasteries, many in what had been Roman frontier forts, especially under Ghassanid Arab rule when the frontier was prosperous and largely peaceful. Following the Arab–Islamic takeover this was no longer a frontier zone, but instead lay at the heart of an expanding empire.

The rival Sassanian Empire witnessed major military, economic and political changes during its last century of existence, not least by building its own frontier fortifications in the Fertile Crescent, facing those of the Romano-Byzantine *limes*. Several were once thought to be Roman, but have since been identified as Sassanian. Meanwhile, there had been a fragmentation of authority within other parts of the Sassanian-Iranian empire, accompanied by the rise of a minor local aristocracy while several frontier provinces achieved considerable autonomy. This certainly had an impact upon the number as well as the construction and design of local fortifications.

The Fertile Crescent, Egypt and Arabia

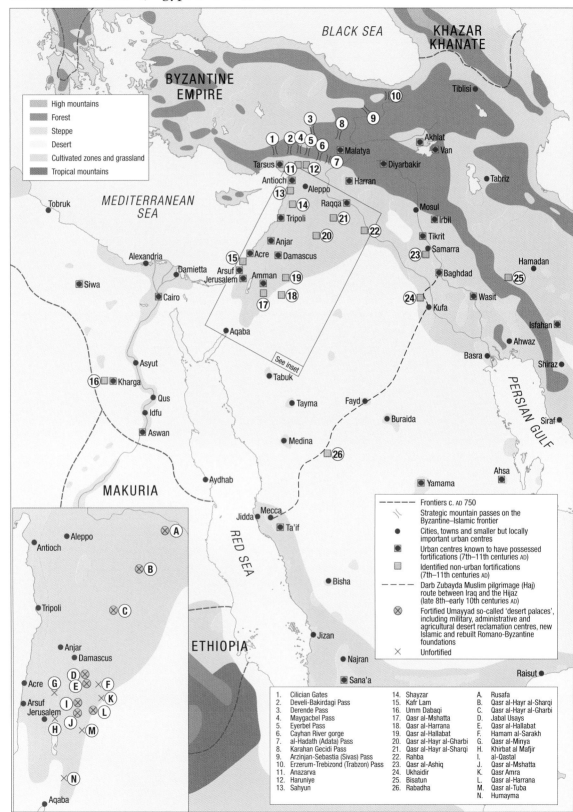

Legend:
- High mountains
- Forest
- Steppe
- Desert
- Cultivated zones and grassland
- Tropical mountains

BLACK SEA

KHAZAR KHANATE

BYZANTINE EMPIRE

Tiblisi

③ ⑧ ⑨ ⑩

① ② ④ ⑤ ⑥

Akhlat
Van

Malatya

⑦

Diyarbakir

Tarsus

⑪ ⑫

Harran

Tabriz

Antioch

⑬

Aleppo

⑭ Raqqa

Mosul

Irbil

Tripoli

MEDITERRANEAN SEA

Tobruk

⑳ ㉑

Tikrit

㉒

Samarra

㉓

Hamadan

Anjar

㉕

⑮ Acre Damascus

Baghdad

Alexandria

Damietta

Arsuf
Jerusalem Amman ⑲

Wasit

Siwa

Cairo

⑰

⑱

㉔

Kufa

Isfahan

Ahwaz

Basra

Shiraz

PERSIAN GULF

Aqaba

See inset

Asyut

Tabuk

⑯ Kharga

Qus

Tayma   Fayd

Idfu

Buraida

Siraf

Aswan

Medina

㉖

Ahsa

MAKURIA

Aydhab

Yamama

Mecca

Jidda

Ta'if

RED SEA

Bisha

Frontiers c. AD 750

Strategic mountain passes on the Byzantine–Islamic frontier

Cities, towns and smaller but locally important urban centres

Urban centres known to have possessed fortifications (7th–11th centuries AD)

Identified non-urban fortifications (7th–11th centuries AD)

Darb Zubayda Muslim pilgrimage (Haj) route between Iraq and the Hijaz (late 8th–early 10th centuries AD)

Fortified Umayyad so-called 'desert palaces', including military, administrative and agricultural desert reclamation centres, new Islamic and rebuilt Romano-Byzantine foundations

× Unfortified

ETHIOPIA

Jizan

Najran

Sana'a

Raisut

Inset map

Aleppo

Antioch

⊗Ⓐ

⊗Ⓑ

Tripoli

⊗Ⓒ

Anjar

Damascus

Acre Ⓖ Ⓓ⊗ ×Ⓕ
        Ⓔ⊗
Arsuf Ⓘ⊗   ×Ⓚ
Jerusalem ⊗   ×Ⓛ
       Ⓗ Ⓙ ×Ⓜ

×Ⓝ

Aqaba

Numbered list

1. Cilician Gates	14. Shayzar	A. Rusafa
2. Develi-Bakirdagi Pass	15. Kafr Lam	B. Qasr al-Hayr al-Sharqi
3. Derende Pass	16. Umm Dabaqi	C. Qasr al-Hayr al-Gharbi
4. Maygacbel Pass	17. Qasr al-Mshatta	D. Jabal Usays
5. Eyerbel Pass	18. Qasr al-Harrana	E. Qasr al-Hallabat
6. Cayhan River gorge	19. Qasr al-Hallabat	F. Hamam al-Sarakh
7. al-Hadath (Adata) Pass	20. Qasr al-Hayr al-Gharbi	G. Qasr al-Minya
8. Karahan Gecidi Pass	21. Qasr al-Hayr al-Sharqi	H. Khirbat al Mafjir
9. Arzinjan-Sebastia (Sivas) Pass	22. Rahba	I. al-Qastal
10. Erzerum-Trebizond (Trabzon) Pass	23. Qasr al-Ashiq	J. Qasr al-Mshatta
11. Anazarva	24. Ukhaidir	K. Qasr Amra
12. Haruniye	25. Bisatun	L. Qasr al-Harrana
13. Sahyun	26. Rabadha	M. Qasr al-Tuba
		N. Humayma

Iran and the Caucasus

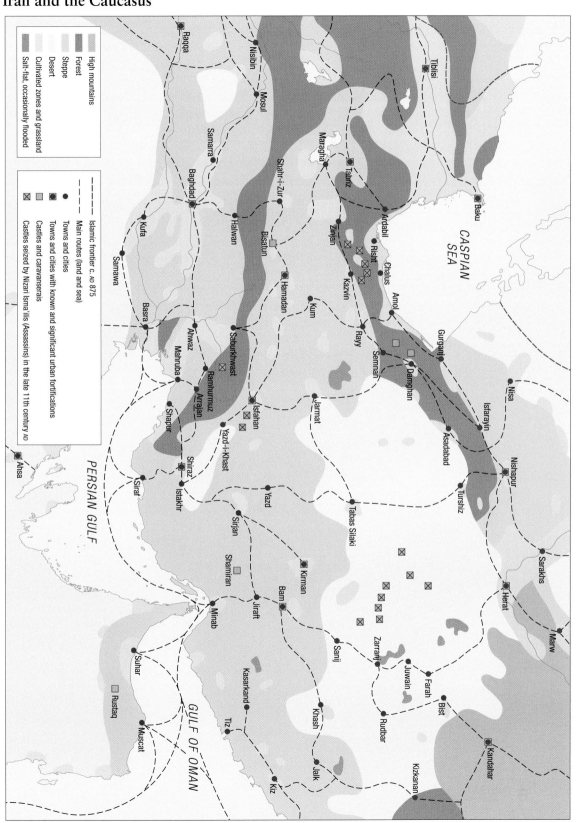

Legend:

High mountains
Forest
Steppe
Desert
Cultivated zones and grassland
Salt-flat, occasionally flooded

– – – Islamic frontier c. AD 875
– – – Main routes (land and sea)
● Towns and cities
● Towns and cities with known and significant urban fortifications
◉ Castles and caravanserais
⊠ Castles seized by Nizari Isma'ilis (Assassins) in the late 11th century AD

CASPIAN SEA

PERSIAN GULF

GULF OF OMAN

Raqqa
Nisibin
Mosul
Samarra
Baghdad
Kufa
Samawa
Basra
Halwan
Shahr-i-Zur
Bisatun
Maragha
Tabriz
Zinjan
Ardabil
Tiblisi
Baku
Risht
Chalus
Kazvin
Amol
Gurganj
Nisa
Hamadan
Kum
Rayy
Semnan
Damghan
Istarayin
Asadabad
Nishapur
Sarakhs
Marw
Herat
Ahwaz
Saburkhwast
Mahruba
Ramhurmuz
Arrajan
Shapur
Isfahan
Jarmat
Yazd-i-Khast
Shiraz
Istakhr
Yazd
Tabas Silaki
Turshiz
Ahsa
Siraf
Sirjan
Shamiran
Kirman
Zaranj
Juwain
Farah
Bist
Kizkanan
Kandahar
Suhar
Minab
Jiraft
Bam
Sanij
Rudbar
Rustaq
Muscat
Tiz
Kasarkand
Khash
Jalk
Kiz

7

Central Asia would play a major role in the development of early medieval Islamic military architecture. This area included territories north and south of the Amu Darya, the ancient Oxus River, the northern regions of present-day Afghanistan and the mountainous lands bordering what is now the Chinese autonomous region of Xinjiang. The defeat and dispersal of Hephthalite 'Huns' around AD 557 had, in fact, resulted in the Turks controlling most territory north of the Amu Darya while the Sassanians took, or at least claimed, areas to the south. Meanwhile, small Hephthalite principalities survived around Kabul in eastern Afghanistan and were still there when the Muslim conquerors overran western Afghanistan in the mid-7th century.

Further north, the later 6th and 7th centuries were marked by an expansion of agriculture and towns between the Syr Darya River and China. Here many Turkish rulers grew rich from trade along the 'Silk Roads' linking China, Iran, the Middle East and Mediterranean Europe, much of their wealth being expended on decorated palaces, urban fortifications and some more isolated castles. It is also important to realize that such regions were not inhabited solely by Turkish nomads. In fact, in many places the population largely consisted of small agricultural communities, often with local fortifications, and small merchant towns which themselves were often fortified.

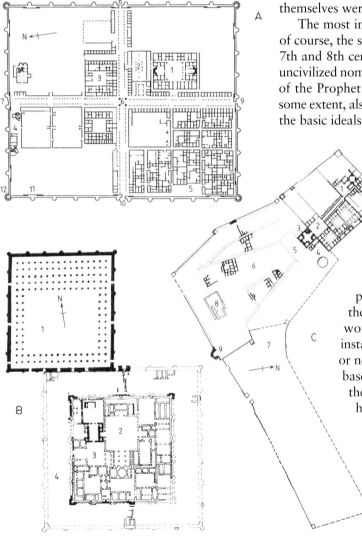

The most important event during this period was, of course, the sweeping Arab-Islamic conquests of the 7th and 8th centuries. These were not an invasion by uncivilized nomadic tribesmen. In fact, the main thrust of the Prophet Muhammad's social message and, to some extent, also his religious message, was contrary to the basic ideals of Bedouin society. Islamic expansion, like Islamic civilization as it evolved in subsequent centuries, was essentially urban.

Fortified cities and towns were important from the very start of Islamic history, the first Muslim armies having to take such places in order to win and maintain control. The invaders not only captured siege equipment, but proved fully capable of using it, and of then defending the fortifications they thus won. Muslim Arab garrisons were soon installed in conquered forts while existing or newly founded towns served as garrison bases for further campaigns. For example, the huge fortified city of Marw on what had been the north-eastern frontier of the Sassanian Empire served just this purpose, especially as the Arabs now faced stiffer resistance from the militarily powerful principalities of Central Asia and Afghanistan. The widespread notion that 19th-century European armies were the first to invade these regions from the west 'since Alexander the Great' is, of course, nonsense. Meanwhile, back in Iraq, Basra was an even more important military base, but, being near the centre of the rapidly expanding Islamic empire, was not thought to require fortifications.

The heroic age of Arab–Islamic expansion largely came to an end during the middle decades of the Umayyad Caliphate and the cultural 'golden age' of the 'Abbasid Caliphate that followed. However, increasing stability did not necessarily mean peace along the frontiers or in the central provinces. Indeed, the struggle between the Islamic states and a gradually reviving Byzantine Empire remained a central feature of Middle Eastern history until the 11th century. Consequently a great deal of fortification, ranging from the small and simple to the huge and complex, became a feature of the Islamic-Byzantine frontier zones, as well as of rear areas on both sides of the border.

The 10th and 11th centuries were a period of cultural and artistic brilliance for Islamic civilization, but they were also a time of sometimes acute political fragmentation. This formed the background to a revival of Byzantine aggressiveness in the Middle East, followed by Seljuk Turkish invasions from the east and eventually European Crusader assaults from the west. As a result, 10th-century Syria, the *Jazira* (Mesopotamia) and several neighbouring areas even including Egypt became exposed, but strongly fortified, frontier zones.

Of course, fortification reflects more than simply the historical circumstances of when and where it was built. Cultural factors also play a significant part. In some ways the early Umayyad caliphs saw themselves as successors of the Romano-Byzantine emperors and continued their policy of erecting splendid imperial monuments. However, this attitude began to change after the defeat of a great siege of the Byzantine capital, Constantinople, in AD 718, with the Umayyad Caliphate turning away from its Mediterranean, Romano-Byzantine heritage towards that of Sassanian Iran. This shift became permanent under the subsequent Abbasid dynasty of caliphs. At least as important were the major changes in Arab–Islamic society and, to a lesser extent, that of other peoples in the Middle East. For example, the traditional pre-Islamic rivalry between the Arab confederations of Qays and Yaman, supposedly northern and southern Arabian tribes, had by the 11th century been replaced by competition between

OPPOSITE PAGE: Umayyad fortified settlements.

A Anjar, the fortified 'new town' founded during the reign of the caliph al-Walid (AD 705–15), but which was destroyed only a few decades later (after H. Salame-Sarkis). 1 – great palace; 2 – mosque; 3 – small palace; 4 – *hamam* (public baths); 5 – housing (excavated); 6 – central junction of main shop-lined roads, with a Roman-style monumental tetrastyle; 7 – north gate; 8 – east gate; 9 – south gate; 10 – west gate; 11 – one of twelve pairs of stairs onto the fortified wall; 12 – one of four hollow corner towers (the other 36 smaller towers, including those flanking the gates, are solid).

B Mosque and fortified Dar al-Imara administrative headquarters of Kufa, Iraq, founded in AD 638, but rebuilt by the governor of Basra in AD 670 (after G. Michell). 1 – mosque; 2 – central courtyard; 3 – fortified inner enclosure; 4 – outer fortifications.

C Citadel of Amman, Jordan, refortified during the late Umayyad period c. AD 725–745, and restored in the 9th–10th century following earthquake damage. The palace complex probably dates from the same period as the Umayyad fortifications (after A. Northedge). 1 – inner courtyard leading to throne room; 2 – outer courtyard; 3 – *hamam* (public baths) and cistern area; 4 – well; 5 – *rahba*, public square; 6 – upper citadel; 7 – lower citadel; 8 – ruined Roman temple; 9 – main gate.

LEFT: The fortress which dominates the town and oasis of Rustaq in Oman is known as the Qal'at al-Kisra or 'Fortress of Chosroes', indicating its probable pre-Islamic Sassanian origins. The inner fortress is a rare example of a simple circuit wall without towers, which was a feature of early medieval Iran and much of Arabia. (Author's photograph)

9

The Eastern Frontier from Central Asia to India

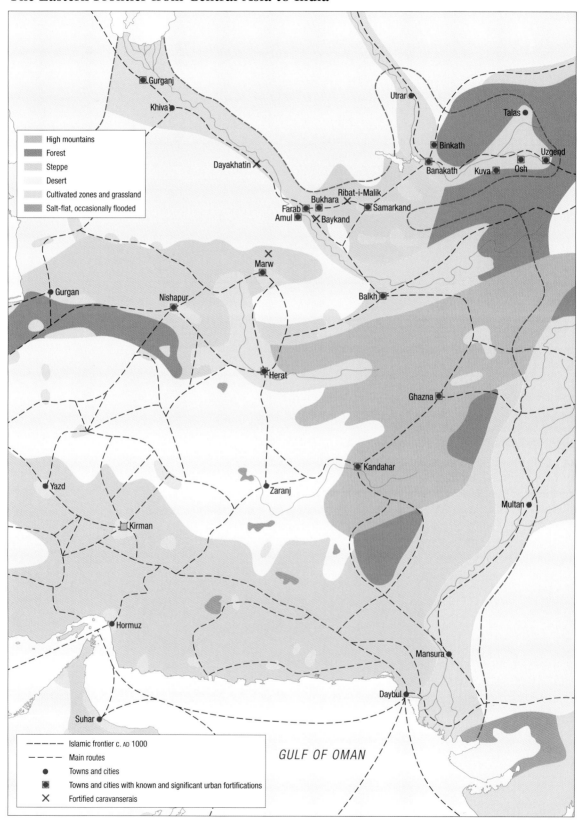

Legend:
- High mountains
- Forest
- Steppe
- Desert
- Cultivated zones and grassland
- Salt-flat, occasionally flooded

Gurganj
Khiva
Utrar
Talas
Binkath
Uzgend
Dayakhatin
Banakath
Kuva
Osh
Ribat-i-Malik
Bukhara
Samarkand
Farab
Amul
Baykand
Marw
Gurgan
Nishapur
Balkh
Herat
Ghazna
Kandahar
Multan
Yazd
Zaranj
Kirman
Hormuz
Mansura
Daybul
Suhar

GULF OF OMAN

- Islamic frontier c. AD 1000
- Main routes
- Towns and cities
- Towns and cities with known and significant urban fortifications
- Fortified caravanserais

10

The most famous Umayyad monuments in Jerusalem are, of course, the al-Aqsa Mosque and the Dome of the Rock on top of the Haram al-Sharif or Temple Mount. However, the Umayyads also constructed a complex of defensible palaces, barracks and perhaps a caravanserai whose partially excavated foundations are next to the domed al-Aqsa Mosque. (Author's photograph)

sedentary and nomadic Arabic-speaking populations, with powerful Arab tribal families erecting castles in the highlands of Syria, Jordan and elsewhere.

The policy of agricultural expansion and new irrigation projects, instigated by the first Umayyad caliph, resulted in regions (which had been devastated by centuries of warfare between the Romano-Byzantine and Iranian empires) beginning to recover. In fact, some of the Umayyad foundations were so ambitious that they might better be described as fortified new towns. Things changed with the fall of the Umayyad dynasty in AD 750, and from then on Syrian cities developed a tradition of opposition to central government, wherever it came from. In this they were helped by their sometimes formidable urban fortifications, but when faced with Bedouin revolts or raids such cities normally rallied to the government because their mercantile populations preferred 'unjust' order to disorder, which interrupted trade.

Once Islamic frontiers had been established in the mid- to late 8th century, their defence was almost entirely based upon fortified cities. This was made easier by the fact that the Islamic Caliphate, having taken over entire states or provinces of existing

Halabiyah was a massive Byzantine fortified town on the river Euphrates, close to the frontier with the hostile Sassanian Empire. When the entire region was united under Islamic rule it became redundant. (Author's photograph)

states, took over existing frontiers. The only notable exception was the Anatolian frontier with a now truncated Byzantine Empire, where virtually new defensive systems and structures had to be developed by both sides.

Fortifications and siege warfare were similarly important in Islam's northern and eastern frontier regions. The process was exemplified in an anonymous Syrian chronicle written in AD 846, which recorded how the Muslim commander Maslamah invaded the lands of the Turks in AD 729 but was defeated. Undaunted, Maslama 'again collected masons and carpenters and he went a second time and fought and won, and he built fortresses and great cities there'.

Jabal al-Qal'a or 'Citadel Hill' dominating the old downtown quarter of Amman, as it appeared when photographed by a Turkish aircraft in 1918. During the Umayyad period, from the late 7th to mid-8th century AD, it was topped by a fortified palace complex and surrounded by a circuit wall. (Courtesy of Royal Jordanian Geographical Society)

DESIGN AND DEVELOPMENT

The early Caliphate and the Umayyad Empire

During the early years of Islamic expansion, Muslim forces used and maintained fortifications that already existed in their newly conquered territories. The first Umayyad caliph, Mu'awiyah, then began refortifying the Mediterranean coasts of the caliphal empire – a process initiated even before he himself became caliph. Nothing much more was done until the reign of the fifth Umayyad caliph, 'Abd al-Malik, who, with his successors, fortified the gradually stabilizing Anatolian frontier. Even so, fixed fortifications never rated highly in the offensive, rather than defensive, military priorities of the Umayyads. This is equally apparent in the first known Arab–Islamic military text, the *Risalah* 'Letters of Advice' written by 'Abd al-Hamid Ibn Yahya shortly before the fall of the Umayyad dynasty. Its military sections placed great emphasis on field fortifications, but not upon permanent fortifications.

Almost all we know about the construction techniques used during this period comes from observation of surviving structures. Nevertheless, it is interesting to note that the best masons of the first Islamic decades were considered to come from Yemen rather than the ex-Romano-Byzantine provinces. Subsequent Umayyad architects used the traditional building techniques of the area in which they worked, and, in Syria, like other western regions, this meant stone. Various masonry styles were available, though the bossed ashlar of earlier Roman centuries had already fallen out of fashion. It is generally thought to have been reintroduced to the Middle East by Western European Crusaders in the 12th century, though there are several examples of its use before the First Crusade. Like the similar style known as rustication, it resulted in a protruding, roughened outer surface that made it more difficult for hurled stones or swinging rams to strike the surface squarely and thus achieve maximum impact.

The first Umayyad caliph Mu'awiyah was credited with introducing baked or fired brick and gypsum mortar to the Islamic Holy City of Mecca, and with bringing the first Persian stonemasons to that area. Meanwhile Iraq's highly developed tradition of brick architecture became ever more sophisticated; examples from the Umayyad period can be found at Wasit and Kufa in the southern part of the country. Farther east, Iran and the Transoxanian provinces of Central Asia both entered an architectural golden age under Islamic rule, baked or fired brick being added to the local tradition of unfired mud-brick architecture. Probably introduced from the Middle East, it was at first used in important structures like mosques, civic buildings and some elements of fortification. Central Asia also saw a continuation of the ancient Turkish tradition of using multiple wooden columns to support the flat roofs of hypostyle halls. Seen in fortified palaces and in mosques, this Central Asian style would eventually be brought west by the Turks and was used in later medieval Anatolia (Turkey).

No Umayyad fortifications retain their crenellations, though several examples of such crestings have been found in their ruins, including this example at Qasr al-Hallabat in Jordan. (Author's photograph)

When it came to design rather than construction, the early Umayyads, as the first imperial dynasty in Islamic history, may have regarded the Roman forts of Syria as the normal plan for princely residences. On the other hand the solid, half-round towers that became a feature of most Umayyad fortifications were a Sassanian Iranian rather than a Romano-Byzantine concept. The idea that such towers had virtually no military value by virtue of being solid is, of course, incorrect. What they sacrificed in internal chambers with embrasures from which arrows could be shot at the enemy they gained in resistance to enemy bombardment. On the other hand, many Umayyad buildings do give an impression that their fortifications were more for show than for use.

The gates of most fortified structures always had some degree of symbolic function, being the most obvious place to demonstrate wealth, strength and the allegiance of those who built them. Gates often also incorporated interesting design features. For example, the earliest Islamic fortifications had simple straight-through gates, but these were normally defended by flanking towers and often by overhanging machicolations, from which missiles or arrows could be dropped or shot at unwelcome visitors.

Suq Ukaz in Saudi Arabia was one of the most important trading centres in the Hijaz region of pre- and early Islamic western Arabia. Its freestone, fortified wall probably dates from the Umayyad or early 'Abbasid late 7th and 8th centuries. (R. Woods photograph)

A THE SMALLER ENCLOSURE AT QASR AL-HAYR AL-SHARQI

The smaller of the two fortified enclosures at Qasr al-Hayr al-Sharqi is the best-preserved Umayyad so-called 'desert castle' or 'desert palace'. This location in the Syrian steppes was probably Zaytuna, a new town built by the caliph Hisham in the early 8th century, though it was never completed. The main structure was of stone and brick. There were 32 courses of masonry with the 29th being slightly thicker than the others. A band of decorative stucco around the gate complex also went around a machicolation immediately above the entrance, though some scholars maintain that this defensive feature was added at a later date. Our reconstruction has also included decorative crenellations based upon those found in the similarly dated 'Hisham Palace' outside Jericho. None survive at Qasr al-Hayr al-Sharqi, though there are signs of where they could have been set. Inset drawing: a reconstructed section of the central courtyard, surrounding arches, two levels of rooms and stairs. The wall-walk was accessed from one of the towers, and the monumental entrance is on the left.

A survey of the most important Umayyad so-called 'desert castles' and fortified buildings farther east shows the variety of architectural styles used during this period. Qasr al-Hayr al-Sharqi is not only the best preserved, but its two walled enclosures and the neighbouring huge *hayr* (game-park, or protected agricultural zone) highlight many of the characteristics as well as the problems associated with Umayyad fortifications. It can probably be identified with Zaytuna, a new town built during the reign of the caliph Hisham. One of the most notable features at Qasr al-Hayr al-Sharqi is the use of stone and brick in one building. However, the basic styles remain Late Antique Mediterranean with few new ideas.

The larger of its two walled enclosures incorporate the most serious elements of fortification. Some towers still have arrowslits in their brick parapets, some positioned so that an archer could shoot along the wall, and all the gates have box machicolations above their entrances, but there is no ditch outside the walls. Nevertheless, these fortifications were not designed to face armies equipped with siege machines.

The walls of both enclosures at Qasr al-Hayr al-Sharqi are relatively thin, the solid towers of the smaller enclosure are no higher than the curtain walls and there may have been no crenellations. The uppermost brick-built levels of the smaller enclosure are almost entirely missing, so it is impossible to know

Ayaz Kala in the Khwarazm region of Uzbekistan, south of the Aral Sea, was a pre-Islamic city that continued to flourish in the first Islamic centuries. Its mud-brick fortifications have the 'corrugated' outer surface, characteristic of much early medieval fortification in Central Asia. (Author's photograph)

The smaller enclosure at Qasr al-Hayr al-Sharqi

Much of the D-shaped fortified city of al-Rafiqa still stands within the modern Syrian town of Raqqa. Founded by the caliph al-Mansur, its most dramatic surviving structure is the brick-built Baghdad Gate, which may have been added in the late 8th century. The exterior was decorated with blind arches (TOP) while the interior was plain (ABOVE). (Author's photographs)

whether these had archery embrasures, and the same may have been the case with other less well-preserved Umayyad castles. Though damaged and partially collapsed, the areas around the central courtyard were originally divided into *bayts*, or units of habitation, usually with latrines. The second storey of this enclosure has largely been lost, but its plan seems to have been the same as the floor below, with latrines immediately above those on the ground floor.

There were 32 courses of stone in the curtain wall, which was about 210cm thick. On the better preserved parts of this outer wall, further courses of moulded bricks survive, with the final six forming a sort of man-high parapet facing the courtyard. There must have been a corresponding parapet on the outside, but only a few fragments remain to indicate that there was a continuous course of brick, then three of stone, then further courses of bricks up to a known total of 24 in the best-preserved place. Faint traces of square stones set into the brick courses hint at the presence of stone buttresses, which are likely to have helped support a now entirely lost wall-heading or crenellation. To quote O. Grabar's detailed study of Qasr al-Hayr al-Sharqi; 'Even a continuous vaulted walkway around the whole building is not excluded, for it would explain the bonds in the corner towers as springing for brick vaults' (*City in the Desert: Qasr al Hayr East*, Cambridge, 1978: 20).

Unfortunately, no comparable building survives in sufficiently good condition to make comparisons of their fortifications. Only the northern half-tower is hollow above the second-floor level, containing a spiral stair, which is the only surviving original method of getting to the top of walls, towers and walkway. Each corner tower is topped with a small domed chamber with windows. The stucco decoration above the gate is interrupted by a stone box machicolation, which is itself supported by three carved stone brackets and has brick and stucco decoration around it.

Clearly the smaller of the two enclosures at Qasr al-Hayr al-Sharqi was not a palace, but may have been a fortified caravanserai. Perhaps other large and monumental Umayyad quasi-fortified buildings were similarly caravanserais, including part of the recently excavated Umayyad structures south of the Haram al-Sharif (Temple Mount) in Jerusalem. On the other hand, all these buildings could be barracks for professional, elite troops or military assembly points for tribal or *jund* provincial armies. Perhaps the larger but less decorated enclosure at Qasr al-Hayr al-Sharqi was for troops, while the smaller and more magnificent was for the ruling or commanding elite.

The Sassanian Empire was gone by the time the Byzantine Empire had been pushed far back from the Fertile Crescent. If Umayyad structures did have a military or quasi-military function, it was probably as assembly points for the caliphs' still largely tribal Arab armies. The more important an Umayyad fortress or palace, the more likely it was to be decorated. Qasr al-Hallabat in Jordan can be taken as an example. Here a Roman and then Ghassanid fortress was made into an Umayyad princely residence, while a mosque was built just outside the fortifications. The palace itself was adorned with stone floor mosaics, like those that had been common throughout the eastern provinces of the Romano-Byzantine Empire, but also by delicate glass wall or ceiling mosaics. Qasr al-Hallabat also had wall paintings and carved stucco decoration, which included elements of Graeco-Roman design.

No major urban fortifications survive from the Umayyad period and almost nothing is known about the defences of Damascus at this time. In fact the city, as capital of the vast Umayyad Caliphate, may already have been overflowing its Roman walls. Smaller-scale examples can be seen at Amman, Anjar and

The Crusader defences of the town of Arsuf in Palestine were, in reality, largely Islamic and dated from the 10th and 11th centuries. (Author's photograph)

Aqaba. Another was at Madinat al-Far, also known as Hisn Maslama or the 'castle of Maslama' 70km north of Raqqa, where excavations show that early medieval written descriptions were remarkably accurate. Development of the site began as an Umayyad irrigation and canal-digging project, a new urban centre being added after the area was fully pacified and was being settled by the Arab conquerors during the reign of the Umayyad caliph al-Walid I. However, the use of the word *hisn* was rare in such Umayyed foundations, and probably highlighted its military function.

The core of the site consists of a square urban plan with curtain walls about 330m along each side, plus four gates symmetrically placed and a moat around the outside. South of the main site are a number of large houses, some on elevated platforms. These houses are enclosed by a weaker wall surrounding a much larger area north of the main town and probably date from the Abbasid redevelopment of nearby Raqqa in the late 8th century. The debris of the city walls and gates suggests that their original height was considerable, especially the ten regularly spaced towers along each side. Much of the wall itself seems to have been of mud brick, while the square northern gate tower was filled with mud brick laid upon one or two layers of limestone. The east gate was more elaborate, having two protruding towers lined with limestone slabs. Its gate room was square and its inner façade was decorated with a limestone lining and fragments of earlier Byzantine architecture.

The remarkable complex of large Umayyad buildings around the south-west corner of the Haram al-Sharif (Temple Mount) in Jerusalem date from approximately the same time as the Aqsa mosque above them, when the Umayyad caliph al-Walid had the entire area redesigned. The central palace was presumably used by the caliph when he visited Jerusalem, while the other building may have included barracks for a garrison. However, this ambitious project did not last long, being badly damaged during an earthquake in AD 748 then demolished by an even worse earthquake in 1033.

Amman was never as important as Jerusalem, but more remains of its Umayyad fortifications. These surround the summit of Jabal al-Qal'a or Citadel Hill, where the remains of an Umayyad palace lie amid an urban complex whose layout and colonnaded streets reflect strong Roman architectural influence. The fortifications themselves follow an earlier Roman line and are

The double wall of Kizil Kala or 'Red Fortress' in Uzbekistan, which gets its name from the colour of its crumbling mud-brick fortifications. It was built before the Arab–Islamic conquest of Central Asia, but remained important until at least the 9th century. (Author's photograph)

entirely built of stone, sometimes regularly laid and incorporating re-used ashlar blocks, but elsewhere constructed in a less ordered way. The wall itself was strengthened by shallow buttresses and had irregularly spaced towers at the gates or corners. The Umayyad towers do not project much beyond this circuit wall, but contained small chambers and were three storeys, 11–12m high. Whether they originally included arrow-slits is unknown.

Aqaba on the Red Sea coast became a *misr* 'camp city' immediately after the Islamic conquest, and remained important until it was sacked during a revolt against Fatimid rule in AD 1024. In fact, the new Islamic walled town of Aqaba may have been founded under the Rashidun caliphs before the Islamic state was taken over by the Umayyad dynasty. Its fortifications were nevertheless real enough and were modified at various times, especially the north-western gate, which was narrowed not long after being built. There were four gates in all, plus boldly projecting D-shaped towers, all of which were hollow in the same style as comparable Roman defences.

In Iraq the early Muslim rulers erected several military or quasi-military buildings. Karkh Fayruz at Samarra was a square fort with a circuit wall of rammed earth about five metres wide, strengthened by regular, half-round solid towers, and is regarded as the only well-preserved, very early Islamic fortification in the eastern provinces. As in Egypt, newly founded early Islamic cities that were not close to external frontiers normally did not have city walls during the Umayyad period. Wasit was an exception. Located on both banks of what was an earlier, though now shifted, course of the river Tigris, it incorporated the small Sassanian town of Kaskar on the east bank, while a settlement on the west bank was entirely new. Both were basically triangular in plan and faced the river. There were no references to fortifications around the ex-Sassanian eastern town, though there were around the new western city. At its heart, next to the river, was a palace or administrative complex, which had a strong outer wall with corner towers. This may have formed a defensible complex whose circuit wall extended to enclose the main mosque, which also had solid towers. The Arab historian Yaqut recorded that the cost of building the walls, main mosque, governmental palace and two moats of Wasit was 43 million *dirhams*, a huge sum at that time.

Much of the Arabian peninsula saw an architectural revolution during the early Islamic period, resulting from the wealth that poured into a region which lay at the cultural, religious and, for a few decades, the political heart of a new superpower. Previous military and other architectural forms such as the *hisn* and *utum* remained, though in finer and more elaborate forms. Those that have been studied in the Hijaz region generally consist of a paved court with a stone curtain-wall set in mortar, a tall stone building, which was presumably the *utum* itself, sometimes crenellated and normally standing at one corner to dominate the whole site. More ambitious civil and military architecture began to appear in Arabia during the reign of the first Umayyad caliph, al-Mu'awiya, who built a powerful fortress at Qasr Khallan near Medina. Other members of the Umayyad elite and aristocracy were responsible for irrigation systems, walled gardens, estates, palaces and forts in various parts of the Hijaz, not least in the Holy Cities of Mecca and Medina themselves.

Most of what is known about smaller frontier defences from this early period comes from written sources. The early Arab historian al-Baladhuri, for example, said that the caliph Hisham was responsible for several fortifications in the northern frontier area of Syria. They are said to have been designed by an architect named Hassan Ibn Mahawayhi al-Antaki, who was probably a

mawali 'client' convert to Islam. Another named architect was Abd al-Aziz Ibn Hayyan al-Antaki Qatarghash, who was credited with fortifying the castles of Murah, Baghras and Buqa. The *rabid* or suburb of Massisah not far from Antioch was similarly fortified while the ship-building arsenal was moved from Acre to Tyre.

In contrast to other obscure and often rebuilt sites, the Umayyad town of Anjar in Lebanon has been extensively excavated. The town is about 310 x 370m, with a single curtain wall with hollow corner towers, eight or ten small, rounded but solid towers along each wall, pairs of which flank the four gates. Nothing remains to indicate wall-head defences, but there are three pairs of stairs giving access to the top of the wall on each side of the city. Farther south the early medieval Palestinian city of Arsuf was a genuine coastal fortification where the persistent threat of Byzantine naval attack led to the population being consolidated into a fortified area about one-third the size of the pre-Islamic city, probably in the late 7th or early 8th century. This was easier to defend and was provided with a city wall strengthened with external buttresses, a surrounding moat and a main gate through the eastern side. At Arsuf the fortified curtain wall was built upon an accumulated bed of sand, even though there was bedrock or solid ground immediately beneath. This was also seen under the domestic buildings and seems to have been designed to limit the shock effects of earthquakes and to enable water to drain away from the foundations.

Another less known example of Umayyad coastal-frontier fortification was excavated at Tocra, in the Libyan province of Barqa (Cyrenaica) neighbouring Egypt. Here, probably in the early 8th century, the Umayyads strengthened what is believed to have been a Byzantine fortified palace or governor's residence by simply adding round corner towers made of rather rough ashlar masonry. Early Islamic fortification in distant and less stable regions of the Caliphal empire

Qasr al-Kharana stands at the junction of several desert routes and was once thought to date from the brief Sassanian occupation of this area in the early 7th century. More recent studies show Qasr al-Kharana to be one of the earliest surviving examples of Umayyad Islamic fortification, built before AD 710. (Author's photograph)

Ribat-i-Malik was the medieval equivalent of a fortified 'motel', built in the mid-11th century to provide merchant caravans and other travellers with secure accommodation. Today only the decorated brick entrance arch survives intact (BELOW), though part of the curtain wall survived long enough to be photographed in the late 19th or early 20th century (BELOW LEFT). (Author's and A.U. Pope's photographs)

The castle of Haruniye takes its name from its founder, the Abbasid caliph Harun al-Rashid – of 'Arabian Nights' fame. Situated on a steep and often cloud-shrouded hilltop, it watched over a strategic mountain pass between Syria and the coastal plain of Cilicia. (Author's photograph)

were noticeably more businesslike. Marw, on the border between Iranian Khurasan and Central Asia, not only lay close to a dangerous frontier, but was also a major garrison centre. Its outer walls enclosed a huge space and were probably the continuously repaired successors of Hellenistic fortifications erected by Alexander the Great's generals centuries earlier. They may have been copied later in the 'long walls' that surrounded the Central Asian oasis of Bukhara and which ran from Samarkqand to the Zarafshan river.

In other respects Marw was a more typical early medieval Islamic eastern Iranian fortified city. Its partially surviving and massive inner fortifications incorporated several features that were characteristic of Central Asian military architecture for centuries. Most striking was the articulated buttressing that looked rather like a sequence of half-round towers, touching each other and giving an almost corrugated effect. The pre- and early Islamic fortified city or *Gyaurkala* of Marw also had a citadel or *ark* (*Erk-kala* in Turkish) on its northern side. A new Islamic city or *shakhristan* soon developed alongside the *Gyaurkala*, but this *Sultan Kala* used essentially the same traditional architectural features, including arrow slits in fortified walls of simple *pakhsa* construction, consisting of large unbaked building blocks of earth and straw.

There were fewer changes in the design of fortified palaces and towns in the farthest eastern frontier provinces. In many respects, these high valleys were only nominally part of the Umayyad Caliphate, though direct Islamic rule, Islamic civilization and the Islamic religion arrived during the 'Abbasid Caliphate. One such transitional building was the royal palace of the *Afshins* or local rulers of Ustrushana, in a fertile valley where the upper Syr Darya River flows out of the Farghana upland valley towards the steppes. According to the Tajik archaeologist N.N. Negmatov:

> The palace consists of a hall with three galleries and throne loggia, small reception room, an oratory, sleeping rooms, living premises, and armoury, corridor, kitchens and bakeries. The interiors of all the ceremonial rooms, locations and corridors were decorated with richly painted polychrome murals, wooden architectural elements, panels and marvellously sculptured friezes'.[1]

Other comparable sites show that the Muslims continued to use and to build tall tower-like fortifications in Central Asia, some to protect major trade routes, others to defend settlements or feudal estates. Another fortress in this region that deserves comment is that of Mug-tepe, which was the main castle of Arslan Tarkan, the local vassal ruler of Farghana. Here archaeologists also found numerous documents, some in Arabic and one being a copy of a letter from the ruler of Panjikath (Penjikent) area to the Arab regional governor in AD 717 or 719. Mug was a small castle in a naturally defensible position with the Zarafshan River to the north and west, while the eastern side was protected by a narrow gorge. The only way up to the castle was by a narrow path from the south-west.

The 'Abbasid golden age
The 'Abbasid dynasty seized control of the Caliphate in the mid-8th century and their reign saw the further spread of Iraqi, Iranian and Central Asian styles and methods of construction. It is also interesting to note Chinese accounts of

1 N.N. Negmatov (tr. D. Nicolle), 'O zhivopisi dvortsa Afshinov Ustrushani (De la peinture du palais royal d'Oustrouchana: Communication Préliminaire)', *Sovetskaya Arkheologiya*, 3 (1973), 183–202.

the presence of Chinese craftsmen in Baghdad during the first year of construction of this new 'Abbasid imperial capital. They are assumed to have been amongst the captives taken by an Arab–Islamic army following its victory over a Chinese army at the Battle of the Talas River in Central Asia ten years earlier. Whether any were involved in military architecture is unknown, but the presence of oriental defensive features would become one of the most interesting aspects of 'Abbasid fortification and surely had some connection with the presence of increasing numbers of Turks, the majority being 'military slaves', known as *ghulams* or *mamluks*, in Abbasid armies across the Middle East. Meanwhile, some of the skills demanded of senior military officers were also expected of the 'perfect secretary' or administrator, according to a text by Ibn Qutaiba written later in the 9th century. Such men should have various practical and engineering skills including experience of the construction of buildings, particularly bridges and aqueducts.

The castle of Qal'at Musa Ibn Nusayr, on a rock overlooking of al-Ula in north-western Saudi Arabia was supposedly built for the Muslim general who conquered Spain and Portugal. It is an early fortress, but was probably restored many times from the start of the 8th century.
(R. Woods photograph)

Despite a westward spread of eastern military and other architectural forms, there were still two distinct traditions when it came to urban fortifications. The Mediterranean continued to be characterized by stone, fired brick and regularly spaced projecting towers, while the Iraqi, Iranian and Central Asian style was typified by massive beaten earth ramparts up to 20m thick. Now, however, a combination of these traditions led to hugely ambitious military and urban architecture using a mixture of fired and unfired brick, often on stone foundations and incorporating stone elements, but with the vertical walls and regularly spaced towers more closely associated with the Mediterranean style.

The most extraordinary of these projects was undoubtedly the Round City of Baghdad itself, founded by the Caliph al-Mansur in AD 762. Its sheer size made the new 'Abbasid caliphal capital a staggering statement of power, wealth and prestige. Sadly nothing now remains of what was essentially two concentric wheel-like areas of housing for military officers, dignitaries and servants. The four main gates in the main outer wall included a bent entrance, or *bashura* in Arabic, which forced an attacker to expose his unshielded right side and hindered a direct cavalry assault if the gate were destroyed. This idea is thought to have been introduced by the new 'Abbasid rulers from Transoxania, where it had been in use for a long time. Normally a *bashura* formed an integral part of a new gate, though it could also be added to old gates as, for example, with the ancient Roman triple entrance *Bab Sharqi* in

B NEXT PAGE: ONE OF THE MAIN GATE COMPLEXES OF THE ROUND CITY OF BAGHDAD

Nothing now remains of the famous Round City, though students of the history of Islamic architecture often hear about the supposed finding of a 'single brick' whose dimensions exactly matched those in medieval Arabic descriptions of the city. These also gave details of the main gates, which incorporated the latest style of bent entrance. The Round City was surrounded by three fortified walls behind which were two rings of offices, barracks, housing and the facilities of a great city. Within these was a huge open space, near the centre of which lay the palace, main mosque and what might have been

barracks for the caliph's immediate guard unit.

Top right inset: a section through the inner domed gate with enclosed 'killing zones' on either side where an attacker could be trapped. The outside of the city is to the right, and the interior with a shop-lined street is to the left.

Lower right inset: a plan view of Baghdad at its greatest extent in the 10th century. It consisted of the Round City surrounded by suburbs, and was bisected by the Tigris and by canals that brought water for drinking and irrigation, as well as transporting food for over a million inhabitants.

Qasr al-Kharana includes several features deriving from Iraqi, Iranian and Central Asian architecture, including stucco surfacing, simple arched squinches and rows of decorative false columns supporting the main arch. (Author's photograph)

the eastern wall of Damascus. Here the southern and central archways were walled up and a *bashura*-style addition was built in front of the remaining northern archway.

A recent interpretation of the detailed but sometimes confusing contemporary descriptions focused on the fortification:

> From the outside these consisted of a ditch and then two lines of walls separated by an open space (*fasil*). The inner wall was lined with round interval towers, which are estimated to have been about 20m high… At the wall-head there were rounded battlements (*sharafat*). There were four gates, each of which consisted of a gate in the outer wall, followed by a passage and then a more elaborate gate in the inner wall, surmounted by a domed chamber at the upper level.[2]

From the start there were additional military cantonments near the Round City, soon followed by civilian suburbs, which eventually resulted in a sprawling metropolis that became the largest city in the world, at least in terms of population. This outer city was still unfortified at the time of the first siege of Baghdad in AD 812/3, during an Abbasid civil war. By the time of the next siege, things had, however, changed:

> The walls had a *khandaq* outside them and shelters (*mizallat*) on the inside for horses to shelter from the sun and rain. Special attention was given to the gates, each one of which had a *dihliz* or covered hallway attached to it where 100 infantry and 100 cavalry could be stationed. The entrance to the Shammasiya Gate was defended by five *shadakha*, which stretched across the road. These were described in the text as made of cross-beams and boards with protruding spikes… It is clear that there were spiked wooden barriers in front of the gate itself and then a hanging gate or portcullis. On the outer gate an *'arrada* [earliest and simplest form of manpowered beamsling stone-throwing machine] was set up and on the inner gate there were five big *manjaniq* [larger but still manpowered beamsling stone-throwing machine]…and six more *'arradat*… The whole programme of fortification must have been completed very rapidly and is said to have cost 330,000 dinars.[3]

South-west of Baghdad in the Iraqi desert stand the two 'desert castles' of Atshan and Ukhaidir. The former might be Umayyad, but Ukhaidir is generally believed to have been built for the 'Abbasid prince Isa Ibn Musa after he went into internal exile around AD 776. Ukhaidir is particularly interesting because it combines poor masonry with very advanced design, and, as such, was typical of many aspects of medieval eastern Islamic fortification. The large fortified enclosure is approximately 170m along each side, the intact parts of the outer wall including the wallhead reaching 17m. Round towers stand at each corner, with ten half-round towers on each side and split or quarter-round towers flanking three of the gates. The outer surfaces of the walls are not flat, but have two pointed blind arches between each tower. The towers themselves are solid, but at the wallhead was a covered walkway that opened into a chamber at the summit of each tower and had slits in the floor, which enabled a garrison to defend the foot of the wall.

2 H. Kennedy, *The Armies of the Caliphs: Military and Society in the Early Islamic State* (London, 2001), 189.
3 *Ibid*, 189.

Mshatta, or the 'Winter Shelter', is one of the Umayyad buildings on the edge of the Jordanian desert that were genuinely palatial. This photograph shows sophisticated Roman-style latrines inside an otherwise solid tower. Mshatta was never completed, and visitors can see where sculptors abruptly abandoned their work, perhaps when the Umayyad dynasty was overthrown in AD 750. (Author's photograph)

The new capital that the 'Abbasid Caliph al-Mu'tasim founded at Samarra in AD 836 developed into another sprawling, but much shorter-lived, metropolis along 50km of the eastern bank of the Tigris north of Baghdad. Here there was no fortified imperial complex. Instead, the palace or palatial complex was surrounded by walls that often had a military appearance but little real military function. Those on the western side of the Tigris were, however, more businesslike, because this area was exposed to raiding (if not full-scale invasion) by dissident tribal groups.

Raqqa, on the north bank of the Euphrates in north-eastern Syria, is the best-preserved example of early medieval Islamic brick-built urban fortification. The actual fortified city should more correctly be called al-Rafiqa, and was founded by al-Mansur ten years after his foundation of Baghdad as a garrison-base for a detachment of the 'Abbasid Caliphate's elite Khurasani–Arab regiments. At the eastern and western ends of the straight wall overlooking the

The art of the Umayyad period included representational styles of carvings that would later become very rare in Islamic civilization. This example was found in the ruins of the main palace in the fortified city of Anjar. It probably represents a hunting rather than combat scene. (Author's photograph)

Anjar is a small, fortified city on the eastern side of the Baqa'a Valley in Lebanon, perhaps intended as a garrison base to protect the Umayyad capital of Damascus. Its fortifications are real rather than symbolic. Here, one of many pairs of stairs from the interior of Anjar leads onto the circuit wall. (Author's photograph)

The Bab al-Amma gate is almost the only part of the huge Jawsaq al-Khaqani fortified palace enclosure at Sammara in Iraq, which remains standing. It was built in AD 836/7 for the 'Abbasid caliph al-Mu'tasim. It consists of three *iwan* (vaulted chambers) made of fired brick. (Author's photograph)

Euphrates were two massive towers, while numerous other smaller, half-round towers were built along the entire curtain wall. Immediately east of the new fortified city of al-Rafiqa there was already a rectangular, originally Hellenistic and now mostly Christian and Jewish town called al-Raqqa. This name would, however, soon be adopted for the entire urban complex.

Harun al-Rashid probably added the second, weaker wall that ran close around the curved part of the city but was farther away from the straight southern wall, thus being in line with the now isolated, free-standing Baghdad Gate. The area enclosed by the two southern walls may have been to

accommodate, protect and control merchant caravans or livestock brought in by neighbouring nomads. Its elongated shape makes it less likely to have served as a *maydan*, or military training ground.

Recent excavation of the collapsed north gate of al-Rafiqa has provided considerable information about the construction of such vital aspects of 'Abbasid military architecture. The fact that its alignment is wrong for the curtain wall may indicate that the gate was built first, and that the overall plan of the city was then slightly modified. It was made of brick upon stone foundations. Within the entrance was a chamber that narrowed at both ends, perhaps indicating that it could be closed with two sets of doors. A suggested reconstruction of the upper chamber, based upon its collapsed elements, implies that there was a room above the first part of the entrance passage, furnished with arrowslits facing outwards plus four slots through the floor and a vaulted ceiling below. A series of small rooms in the curtain wall immediately to the west and partially within the gate-tower were entered from the interior of the city, and may have been *mizallat* to shade the guards or their horses.

Few fortifications survive from the 'Abbasid period in western Syria, Lebanon or Palestine. However, Ibn Tulun, the autonomous ruler of Egypt, was so impressed by the fortifications of the strategic city and harbour of Tyre that he decided to raise Acre to the same condition in the second half of the 9th century. His work included a new eastern mole, which was at least partially constructed by building on top of a great raft which, when heavy enough, sank into the sand beneath. The rest of the mole was then built on top of this remarkable foundation. The 'Tower of the Flies' in the middle of the Bay of Acre was also rebuilt during the early Islamic period, using ashlar masonry fastened together with iron clamps in the ancient Roman manner. It then served as a lighthouse and checkpoint.

Kfar Lam (Ha-Bonim in Hebrew) is a much smaller fortification, but is also better preserved and dates from the early 'Abbasid or late Umayyad period. It stands on the low coastal ridge of central Palestine, has a slightly irregular trapezoid plan and a single narrow entrance with a pointed arch between half round turrets. The rampart wall of Kfar Lam, from 1.6 to 2.8m thick, has four solid cylindrical corner towers and 18 square but irregularly spaced buttresses. Six vaulted rooms have been found inside the fort, though others may subsequently have been demolished, while two pear-shaped water cisterns hewn from the rock were coated with waterproof plaster.

The fortified buildings at way-stations along the Darb al-Zubaydah pilgrimage route between Iraq and the Hijaz were small and simple. This structure excavated at al-Rabadhah consists of an irregular rectangle with one entrance and a courtyard. One larger tower may have been strengthened when the Darb Zubaydhah was under attack by Qarmatian 'fundamentalists' during the 10th century. (Al-Ansari photograph)

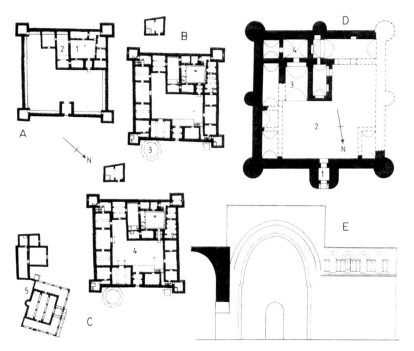

Umayyad 'desert palaces' in the Fertile Crescent.

A–C: the development of Qasr al-Hallabat, Jordan (after I. Arce).

A – Late Roman *Limes Arabicus quadriburgium*, 4th–5th centuries AD. B – Ghassanid Arab *praetorium*, 6th century following earthquake of AD 551. C – Umayyad palace and mosque, 7th–8th centuries AD, destroyed by an earthquake in AD 748/9. 1 – original Roman 2nd-century AD fort enclosed by later Roman fortifications; 2 – enlargement of Roman fort in the 2nd or 3rd century AD; 3 – cistern; 4 – Umayyad palace; 5 – Umayyad mosque outside the fortifications.

D–E: early Islamic Qasr Atshan, Iraq, probably first half of the 8th century AD (after B. Finster). D – plan. E – façade of the Iwan, vaulted reception hall. 1 – gate; 2 – courtyard; 3 – Iwan; 4 – inner chambers.

Written sources confirm that the early 'Abbasid caliphs put considerable effort and money into the fortification of their frontier with the Byzantine Empire. Nevertheless their quality varied, the urban defences of Malatya being rebuilt with good-quality stone whereas al-Hadath was initially constructed of mud brick, which disintegrated in ferocious winter rains. Much of the actual building work was done by the garrisons themselves, though there are also references to the recruitment of professional *fa'ala* craftsmen. During the rebuilding of Malatya in AD 757 special rewards were offered for those who 'reached the battlements' first, or in other words completed their allotted section of wall. Perhaps as a result, this massive but strategically vital exercise was completed in only months.

The caliph Harun al-Rashid was responsible for repairing the defences of Adana, Misis and Anarzarbus (Ayn Zarba). At the latter, his work in AD 796 replaced the ancient Roman walls with a shorter circuit enclosing a smaller and more defensible area. A little over 50 years later the caliph al-Mutawakil's builders were active at Anarzarbus, an inscription bearing his name being found in the ruins of a tower just outside the west gate.

The best preserved of these early medieval Islamic frontier forts in southern Turkey is, however, Haruniye. Named after Harun al-Rashid, it had been completed by AD 786, securing a strategic route across the mountains between Maras and the Cilician Plain. Haruniye is perched on an almost pointed outcrop of rock overlooking what is now a barely used trail through a cleft in the Nur Daglari Mountains. It is also visible from the fort at Cardak Kalesi and may once have formed part of a chain of such forts along the mountains.

The first autonomous and, in practical terms, effectively independent Islamic ruling dynasty in Egypt was that of the Tulunids. They established the new military cantonment of Qata'i north of the early Islamic 'barracks city' of Fustat, in the south of what is now Cairo. Though Qata'i was never fortified, and seems to have been modelled upon the similarly unfortified 'Abbasid capital of Samarra, Ibn Tulun feared an 'Abbasid attempt to retake control and so built a fort on nearby Jazira island in the Nile.

The only serious fortifications that are known to have existed in early Islamic Egypt were on the Mediterranean coast, and were in response to a continued Byzantine naval threat. The town and port of Tinnis, on a small island in the coastal lagoon of Lake Manzalah, was, for example, fortified in AD 844. This work was completed in AD 853/4 under Caliph al-Mutawakil who also fortified the ports of Dimyat (Damietta) and Farama (Pelusium). Tinnis eventually had 19 gates and covered at least 93 hectares. A recent survey indicated that the enclosure wall had horseshoe towers at regular intervals, and at the north-eastern corner of the town the wall was found to be a massive doubled structure with what seemed to be smaller interconnecting walls, perhaps originally supporting a broad walkway or fighting platform above. Meanwhile, at the north-west corner there are the remains of a harbour channel, which was again fortified by a round tower.

The supply of drinking water was a major concern, and at Tinnis this was resolved in an unusual way, reflecting the island town's distinctive circumstances. Cisterns built in the 9th century were located deep underground, and had multiple vaults made of brick with their inner surfaces covered in waterproof lime plaster to collect the annual Nile flood.

In Iran the design and construction of urban curtain-walls remained largely unchanged. The basic plan was usually round or rectangular. Although small cities commonly used only two or three gates, the coming of Islam and the economic expansion that followed often resulted in the opening of additional gates. Usually known simply as the New Gate, they can be found at Zaranj, Isfahan and elsewhere. There was a comparable decline in the importance of 'cosmological' urban plans with gates at the points of the compass. Instead, the layout of cities generally became more pragmatic.

Unfortunately, little remains of this region's abundant military architecture described in contemporary sources in the 9th and 10th centuries. At first mud brick was the most common building material, but by the end of the 10th century baked brick dominated the construction of major buildings. The distinctive 'corrugations' remained a popular style for the outer surface of substantial or fortified walls, while stucco was still the main form of decoration, along with some wall-painting. Meanwhile, an increasing number of more or less fortified caravanserais along the main trade routes further emphasized the mercantile rather than military character of this part of the Islamic world.

Military defences were, of course, still required, especially in strategic communications and garrison centres such as Marw, but even here the old walled enclosure was gradually abandoned in favour of unwalled suburbs west of the original city. These would not be surrounded by fortifications until the establishment of the Great Seljuk Sultanate in the late 11th century. In exposed frontier areas, military architecture remained more overt. For example, the ancient town or *shakhristan* of Kahkakha in Tajikistan had remained important even after the removal of the local autonomous but non-Islamic rulers. The pre-Islamic temple became a mosque and the town was divided into two by a wall, the main defended part on the west side consisting of guard buildings, barracks, a *maydan* training ground and a reservoir. In the ruins of its palace archaeologists also discovered no fewer than 5,000 stone balls weighing from 32 to 48kg, intended to be shot by mangonels. It was, of course,

Frontier defences.
A: the fort of Kafr Lam on the Mediterranean coast south of Haifa, early Islamic period but strengthened in the 9th or 10th century AD (after H. Barbe et al.). 1 – pre-Islamic Romano-Byzantine structures; 2 – Crusader chapel with apse cut into wall of fort; 3 – later Islamic structures from Ottoman period.
B: fortress of Anavarza (Arabic: Ayn Zarba), in the frontier zone between the Islamic and Byzantine empires, strongly refortified by the 'Abbasid caliph Harun al-Rashid in AD 796 and again by the Hamdanid ruler of Aleppo in the 10th century AD. 1 – largely abandoned pre-Islamic lower city; 2 – lower castle surrounded by fortifications on northern and eastern sides, by sheer cliffs on southern and western sides; 3 – surviving gate of lower castle, probably 'Abbasid late 8th century AD; 4 – walls and towers largely rebuilt in 12th–13th centuries AD; 5 – first entrance complex to upper citadel, strengthened during Armenian period; 6 – second entrance complex, probably Islamic 8th to 10th centuries AD; 7 – upper citadel.
C: twin citadels of Uzgen, Kyrgyzstan, capital of the Fargana Valley under the Qarakhanids, 11th century AD (after E. Esin).

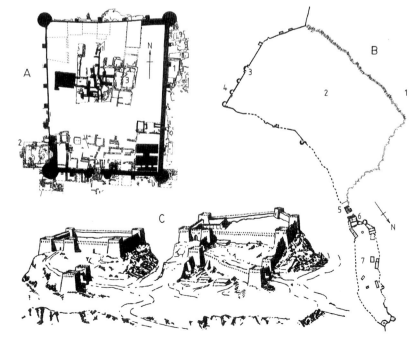

The north side of the court of honour in Ukhaidir before the massive restoration of recent years. It led to the main gate, which was itself set between massive rectangular towers. (Iraqi Ministry of Tourism photograph)

from these eastern regions that the beamsling stone-throwing siege machine, known in Arabic as a *manjaniq* and to modern historians as a mangonel, spread westwards just as the first Arab-Islamic armies were pursuing their conquests eastwards.

Even closer to the tense easternmost frontier lay the fortified city of Kuva, high in the Farghana Valley. According to al-Istakhri, writing in the late 9th or very early 10th century Kuva was situated very favourably:

> There is a *kukhendiz* (citadel), a *shakhristan* (fortified city) and a *rabid* (surburb). The *kukhendiz* had been destroyed. The mosque is situated in the *kukhendiz*. The bazaar, the palace of the ruler and the prison are situated in the *rabid*. The *rabid* is surrounded by the wall, has beautiful gardens, and abundant running water.

Modern archaeological excavations show that the *shakhristan* fortified inner city reached its final form during the medieval period, and was surrounded by thick defensive walls made of typically Central Asian *pakhsa*, or large building blocks of earth and straw.

Taken together, the *shakhristan* and *ark* of Kuva cover approximately 12 hectares and have a strong defensive wall on four sides. The result was an undoubtedly secure location, but one that soon seems to have become crowded, resulting in the development of the *rabid* or suburb in the 9th century. Meanwhile the *shakhristan* continued to be divided into quarters, which were themselves subdivided into houses and small open spaces. Each quarter was home to a particular economic or professional activity, with the glassblowers living in the eastern part, and the potters in the west. In ancient times small canals brought water to the walled *shakhristan*, but as the city flourished and the ground level rose, the population had to get drinking water from wells inside the city walls, though the piped sewerage system still worked.

The defences around the *shahkristan* of Kuva remained in use through the 9th century and had a total length of roughly 1.3km. Two rectangular towers in the north wall were again made of *pakhsa* and had arrow-slits at lower floor level. More recent excavations of the south wall uncovered two further towers, probably from the 10th century, but this time without loopholes. The gates that have so far been studied in the curtain wall were strongly built with entrances that were initially 4.5m wide. The entrances were framed by large timbers to which the gates were attached, it not being practical to hang heavy doors directly from a mud-brick structure. Elsewhere in the medieval Islamic world, this problem was often solved by adding an archway of fired brick.

Other castles in the lowland regions of Central Asia date from the fragmentation of 'Abbasid authority in the 9th and 10th centuries, and several have similarities with Umayyad so-called 'desert castles' in Syria and Jordan. Most have been interpreted as residences of a local aristocracy of *dihqans* who owned most of the land and to whom the local peasantry looked for leadership and protection. The small examples look rather like medieval European-style donjons or keeps, though the upper parts of their curtain walls often consisted of characteristically Central Asian 'corrugated', adjoining semi-circular towers. Some had a central courtyard surrounded by living quarters; others had a large central domed room with vaulted halls on the sides, sometimes decorated with wall paintings.

The large, decorated and strongly fortified caravanserais that are found along almost all the main trade routes of medieval Islamic Central Asia mostly date from after the period under consideration, though a few may even have been present as early as the 9th century. One such stands in the *rabid* or suburb of Daya Khatyn on the west bank of the Amu Darya River, in a settlement that was originally named Tahiriya after its early 9th-century founder. While the original settlement was defended by simple clay walls over 100m long, and dates from the 9th and 10th centuries, there is debate about the caravanserai itself. Perhaps its basic fortified structure and plan were from around the same time as the fortified site, while its magnificent decorated façade was added at a later date. The courtyard was surrounded by *iwans* or deep-set arches, a series of vaults and domes, warehouses and other rooms.

A remarkably complete, mud-brick fortress in the deserted oasis of Ayn Umm al-Dabaqi in Egypt probably dates from between the 10th and 12th centuries. It certainly includes features that are more advanced than those seen in pre-Islamic desert frontier forts. (Author's photograph)

Fragmentation and fortification

Concern for fortification clearly increased across the medieval Islamic world as the power of the 'Abbasid Caliphate waned, political authority became fragmented and several neighbouring states began to take advantage of Islam's military weakness. This was particularly obvious in eastern Anatolia and the Fertile Crescent, where the Byzantine Empire launched a prolonged offensive. Meanwhile, rivalry between Islamic power centres and the rise of rival Caliphates, most notably that of the Fatimids, resulted in a comparable concern for effective fortifications deep within the Islamic world.

By the 10th and 11th centuries Islamic civilization was technologically amongst the most advanced in the world, with sophisticated engineering and architectural skills available for military as well as civil purposes. Various surveying devices were described in detail in engineering treatises, although interest tended to focus on complex machinery and the design of toys for wealthy or political elites. They rarely concerned themselves with everyday working machines. Nevertheless, a combination of need and capability meant that most medieval Islamic towns had mighty walls, towers and gates, the latter often also being decorated.

When the Central Asian scholar and traveller Nasir-i Khusrau visited the Middle East in the mid-11th century, he described its sophisticated military architecture in some detail, showing that in most cases this placed great emphasis on providing raised platforms for archers and defensive siege machines. Having been for centuries a tense frontier region between the Islamic Caliphate and the Byzantine Empire, eastern Anatolia had seen the building of impressive fortifications. In the middle, though generally under Islamic suzerainty, were the Armenians whose builders continued to develop several aspects of Umayyad military architecture that had been dropped by the 'Abbasids. The Armenians also earned a reputation for fine masonry, and these skills would soon be in demand outside their own homeland.

The Hamdanid dynasty that ruled northern Syria, part of northern Iraq and much of south-eastern Turkey in the 10th century inherited militarized regions of what had been the 'Abbasid Caliphate's *thughur al-Jayirah*.

Within the enclosure wall of the Abbasid coastal fort of Kfar Lam, south of Haifa, are a number of chambers, which survived in good condition because they remained useful long after the fortifications had fallen out of use. Some were probably stables for the garrison's horses. (Author's photograph)

This included the fortresses of Zibatra, Hisn Mansur, Mar'ash, al-Haruniyya, al-Kanisa, Ayn Zarba, and the *thughur al-Shami*, which included the fortresses of Massisah, Adana and Tarsus. It was from this period that we have a detailed description of the fortifications, garrison and military organization of Tarsus, written by Abu Amr Uthman al-Tarsusi around the time the city fell to the Byzantines in AD 965. Tarsus stood within two walls, each with five iron gates. Those in the outer wall were 'covered in iron', while those of the inner wall were 'completely of iron'. The inner wall had 18,000 *shurafa* 'vantage points' or crenellations, where 16,000 archers could be stationed. Quite what the remaining 2,000 *shurafa* were intended for is not explained. There were 100 *burj* towers in the inner wall, three of them for *h-r-ri* (vowels unknown) *manjaniq*, which might be the earliest known reference to the counterweight rather than man-powered type. Twenty towers were for large but otherwise normal *manjaniqs*, while another twenty were for *'arradat*, the simplest form of man-powered mangonel. The rest were to be manned by men armed with *qisiyy al-rijl*, small hand-held and 'foot-spanned' crossbows as distinct from the large *charkh* crossbow spanned with a winch. These towers were owned by individual citizens and were either inhabited by permanent residents, temporary warriors or volunteers, or were used as workshops.

Some medieval Islamic fortifications in the Middle East were decorated with carved animals and other motifs as well as Arabic inscriptions. Those seen here are on the 'Dark Gate' of Diyarbakr, which was substantially rebuilt during the 11th century. (Author's photograph)

The Hamdanids were equally famous as patrons of the arts, especially poetry, and a great deal of the Arabic verse written during the reign of Sayf al-Dawla (AD 944–67) dealt with warfare against the Byzantine Greeks. For example, one of al-Mutanabbi's works recorded Sayf al-Dawla's successful restoration of the citadel of Maras in AD 952. It had been destroyed by the Byzantines, and the rebuilding could be completed only following the defeat of an enemy army.

> How the fortress wall rises as though from its crest
> Down to its base it penetrated the stars above and the earth below.
> Violent winds avoid the fortress in fright,
> Birds dare not therein peck the grain.
> Short-haired steeds gallop over the surrounding mountains,
> When like a cotton-carder cold winds scatter snow on their tracks.
> How strange it is that men deem it strange
> That he [Sayf al-Dawla] could build Mar'ash.
> Away with their suspicions!

Archaeological investigation has identified some Hamdanid work by its design and masonry, as well as occasional dedicatory inscriptions. For example, Anazarva (Anarzarbus, 'Ayn Zarba) flourished under Hamdanid rule and the restoration of its defences cost Sayf al-Dawla 3,000,000 *dirhams*. Not far away, much of the structure of Haruniye castle almost certainly dates from Hamdanid restoration in AD 967. Its plan was unlike any other in Cilicia or the surrounding mountains, being a compact walled enclosure with a substantial tower at the east end. Continuous galleries defended the vulnerable north and west flanks, whereas the east and south are protected by a steep escarpment. The embrasures in the 'shooting gallery' are the only confirmed Arab examples from this period, while their particularly deep and broad interiors could be evidence of the use of large *jarkh* crossbows, which were sometimes mounted upon pedestals. In contrast, the massive tower next to Haruniye's eastern gate is covered with smooth basalt ashlar with a single decorative band of limestone. At the base is a thin talus – an anti-mining device that originated in the Islamic Middle East.

THE 'ABBASID DESERT-PALACE OF UKHAIDIR

Ukhaidir was probably built in the late 770s AD, and combines poor masonry with scientific design. A large fortified enclosure surrounds a smaller one that has round towers at each corner, with half-round towers on each side and split towers flanking three of the four gates. A covered walkway on top of the fortified wall opens into chambers at the summit of each tower and has slits in the floor, which enabled a garrison to defend the foot of the wall. These walkways may originally also have had arrow slits facing outwards and sideways. The gates of Ukhaidir consisted of vaulted halls, above which were two levels of chambers like those in the Round City Baghdad, though here they are vaulted rather than domed. An inner chamber in front of the main gate could be shut with a portcullis to trap anyone attacking the door itself. The fortifications of Ukhaidir were considerably more developed than anything from the Umayyad period, while the sumptuous palace and courtyards at the heart of the complex were firmly within an Iranian palatial tradition.

Inset plans top left: the fortified palace was subsequently surrounded by a much larger walled enclosure, highlighted in blue, one wall and gate of which was attached to the first enclosure. There were several courtyards, the largest and most magnificent of which was in the centre. To the right is a plan of one corner of the inner complex, showing archery embrasures facing outwards and inwards.

Top right inset: (left) a vertical section through the curtain wall; (middle) a vertical section through a wall-tower; (right) a vertical section through a corner-tower.

Possible supports for a wooden floor can be seen inside the tower, which was probably topped by a wooden roof.[4]

In the Jazira region between the rivers Euphrates and Tigris the designers of fortifications absorbed ideas from many places, distant and local. Harran, for example, was also one of the last major outposts of the pre-Islamic, indeed pre-Christian, Sabaean religion, and a large Sabaean temple stood in the south-eastern corner of the fortified city until AD 1032 when it was taken over by the local Shi'a Muslim community for use as a fortress. Militarily, the most important relic from early medieval Harran is the south-eastern gate of the citadel. Later embedded within a larger gate, the 11th-century entrance had a horseshoe arch flanked by two solid, rectangular towers; the entire structure was faced with basalt. Several carved panels of inscription were found, and the pillars of the gate were decorated with pairs of hunting dogs, while above were carved birds, probably eagles with folded wings.

Two other examples of urban fortification from this period are found at Diyarbakr in south-eastern Turkey and Marw in Turkmenistan. At Diyarbakr the walls and a citadel in the north-eastern corner of the city rest upon late classical foundations, and are a continuation of that pre-Islamic heritage. On the other hand, Diyarbakr also has an abundance of carved decoration and

The south-eastern gate of the fortified *shakhristan* or inner city of the 10th- or 11th-century Central Asian Islamic frontier city of Kuva in Uzbekistan was of mud brick, and had several features in common with the westernmost forts of China's Great Wall on the other side of the Tien Shan Mountains. (Author's photograph)

4   R.W. Edwards, *The Fortifications of Armenian Cilicia* (Washington, 1987), 30–31.

The 'Abbasid desert-palace of Ukhaidir

The chamber that ran inside the main wall around the smaller fortified enclosure at Qasr al-Hayr al-Sharqi incorporates both stone and brickwork, the masonry being used for the walls whereas the vaulted roof is of brick. (Author's photograph)

inscriptions from the Islamic period, which, like the massive fortifications themselves, reflected the city's huge trading wealth. The Persian-speaking Central Asian traveller Nasir-i Khusraw visited the city in the mid-11th century and described it as the greatest of all fortifications. Behind the crenellations of the main wall was a passage in which an armoured man could move around, stand upright and fight with ease, and there is a space 15 cubits wide between the inner and outer fortifications. Nasir-i Khusraw also maintained that Diyarbakr had four gates that 'included no wood', while outside the main ramparts was another fortification made in the same way as the main wall, with tall watchtowers 'ten cubits high'.

Further south, the coastal city of Tripoli was almost as strong, according to Nasir-i Khusraw: 'Along the battlements are placed *'arradah* [stone-throwing machines] for their fear of the Greeks who are wont to attack the place in their ships'. In contrast, Damascus still seems to have lacked substantial fortifications. Al-Muqaddasi, who came from not far away in Jerusalem, stated that it was only defended by a mud-brick wall in the 10th century, though this was hurriedly repaired when a Fatimid army threatened Damascus in AD 981/2. Jerusalem suffered a significant decline under 'Abbasid rule, and its fortifications were so neglected that Bedouin were able to overrun the place during various revolts against the central government. Large parts may have been derelict even before Jerusalem was struck by a major earthquake in AD 1033, after which the walled area was considerably reduced when the Fatimid caliph al-Zahir had the fortification repaired the following year.

Not surprisingly, a fragmentation of authority resulted in an increase in the importance of smaller, more isolated castles such as Rahba next to the Euphrates. It was restored in AD 968/9, but it is unclear whether this referred to the castle on the edge of the escarpment or to the ramparts of the town of Rahba Malik Ibn Tawq (now Mayadin) on the edge of the river. What is clear is that the Arab tribal chiefs or local rulers who now dominated most of the fertile regions of Syria, Jordan and Lebanon's Baqa'a, as well as the semi-desert steppes to the east, had numerous castles. One of their functions was to resist fundamentalist Qarmathian raiders from deeper inside Arabia, though the hilltop forts built as refuges by the Banu Kilab tribal leaders in much of 11th-century Syria and Jordan were also part of a general process of sedentarization by such Arab tribes.

By the 9th or 10th century, when the surviving walls, towers and entrance gate of Kfar Lam were renovated, the old Romano-Byzantine tradition of mixed brick and stone had largely been abandoned by the Muslim military architects of Syria. (Author's photograph)

After centuries when Egyptian fortifications were limited to a few, mostly coastal, parts of the country, there was a fundamental change of military priorities in AD 969 when Egypt became the power base for a new Shi'a Islamic dynasty with ambitions to replace the existing Sunni 'Abbasid Caliphate. The Fatimids also faced ferocious hostility from the Qarmathians of Arabia, who, though themselves enemies of the 'Abbasid Caliphate, similarly refused recognition to the Fatimids.

Egypt was actually conquered by the Fatimid caliph's *wazir* or 'chief minister', Jawhar, and, while still involved in building a new caliphal palace-city later known as *al-Qahira* (Cairo), he erected a massive field fortification to protect the main construction site from Qarmathian attack. This involved a ditch or fosse being excavated from the Muqattam Hills and Munyat al-Asbagh on the Nile. Ten cubits deep and ten wide, it was crossed by a single bridge and had two gates, whose doors were taken from the perhaps fortified *maydan* cavalry training ground of the Fatimids' Ikhshidid predecessors. Work was, in fact, completed in time to face a Qarmathian attack, which was defeated by a Fatimid sortie after three days' fighting. In AD 974 the Qarmathians attacked again, and this time broke through, but by then al-Qahira itself was strong enough to hold out.

Nothing has yet been found of the first mud-brick wall of al-Qahira, though we do have an account of its foundation in AD 969. This described the *ikhata*, or process of marking out the line of the foundations. After these were excavated, an enclosure of sun-dried bricks or *labin* was erected, part of which was still visible in AD 1400. According to al-Maqrizi, a reliable late 14th-century observer who saw these remains, the bricks were one cubit long by two-thirds of a cubit wide. The width of the circuit wall enabled bodies of troops to move rapidly from one section to another, and permitted enough men to gather at one spot to defeat an enemy assault.

However, a book on warfare by the late medieval Mamluk scholar al-Ansari maintained that the western wall of Fatimid al-Qahira 'was not a [suitable] fortification because it was built upon a low place'. Like the famous (lost) Round City of Baghdad, the Fatimid caliphs' fortified enclosure contained the palace, government offices and barracks for elite garrison regiments. There was also a treasury, a mint to make money, a library, an imperial mausoleum, an arsenal, stables and various other vital facilities. According to Ibn Duqmaq,

The windows of the early 8th-century Umayyad desert fort of Qasr al-Kharana in Jordan cannot have served as arrow slits. Even where they can be reached from inside the building, as here, the 'arc of fire' is too narrow to be militarily useful. (Author's photograph)

Jawhar 'built palaces for his master so that he and his friends and their armies were separate from the general public'. This had, of course, been customary since 'Abbasid times when the old, more open if not necessarily more democratic Umayyad palace organization was abandoned.

The first name given to the new Fatimid palace-city was al-Mansuriya, 'The Triumphant' or 'The Subjugator' – but Egypt's capital is called al-Qahira, or Cairo to English-speakers. This name reflects a story that might be a myth, but which soon caught the popular imagination, and concerned the selection of a moment which astrologers announced would be propitious for work to begin on its walls. Consequently, all along the line of trenches for its foundations a series of wooden posts were connected by cords. Suspended from these cords were bells, so that on the exact moment of 'good fortune' the cords would be pulled, the bells would ring and the workmen could immediately start putting in stones and mortar, which stood ready. According to this legend, however, a crow landed on the cord, the bells tinkled and work began during the night – before the correct time. At this moment the planet Mars was ascendant, and in the Arabic terminology of the time this was *Qahir al-Falak* or 'the Ruler of the Sky', which supposedly led to the new palace-city being known as *al-Qahira*. What is true is that the work of surveying was done in such haste that the rectangular outline was skewed.

The western wall ran parallel to a *khalij* or canal that was medieval Cairo's main source of drinking water, though at a short distance from it. According to al-Maqrizi, there were originally eight gates into this fortified palace complex, some foundations of which have been uncovered, as well as those of small postern gates, which being only about one metre wide were for military purposes. The fact that some, and perhaps all, of these first gates were decorated with Kufic Arabic inscriptions shows that this cannot have been constructed solely of mud brick like the first circuit wall.

Potentially one of the most interesting pieces of medieval military architecture in Egypt is the fortress at Umm Ayn Dabaqi. It dominates an uninhabited oasis north of the great oasis of Kharga, and consists of a high walled enclosure with rectangular corner towers. Because of its isolation,

The fortified old city of Samarkand was known as Afrasiayab in pre- and early Islamic times, but was abandoned after the Mongol conquest in the 13th century. This massive mud-brick structure overlooking the gorge of the small Siab River was the citadel, which still contains two levels of halls, corridors and rooms. (Author's photograph)

The straight, southern side of the D-shaped fortified palace-city of al-Rafiqa (Raqqa) in eastern Syria overlooks a slope from the plateau down to the marshy floor of the Euphrates valley. This was presumably why the architects did not add a moat like that which surrounded the rest of the defences. (Author's photograph)

much of this remarkable castle survives almost to its original height and is dramatic testimony to what can be done with unfired mud brick in a location that hardly ever sees rain.

Madina Sultan in neighbouring Libya is very different. Located between the two main zones of Libya, where the trans-Saharan caravan trade route from Chad reached the Mediterranean, it had a city wall by the 10th century. However, the fortified town of Madina Sultan is set back from the Mediterranean coast, with an outer wall reinforced by a few widely spaced towers, the strongest part of these defences facing the sea, from where piratical attack might be expected. Madina Sultan also had two internal forts while a third fort stood on its own between the town and the shore.

Not far away is Ajdabiyah, which contains a *qasr* fortified palace. The latter was probably built in AD 972 when the Fatimid caliph was transferring his residence from Mahdia in Tunisia to his new caliphal palace-city of al-Qahira in Egypt. This *qasr* is quite small, only 33 by 25m, with hollow, round corner towers and hollow square salients or towers to strengthen the side walls. There is also a monumental entrance similar to that of the Great Mosque in Mahdia and incorporating a bent entrance. On each side of the courtyard were long gallery-like rooms for bodyguards or retainers, while at the other end of this courtyard was a suite of rooms entered through a cross-hall or ceremonial reception chamber. Presumably the site of Ajdabiyah was also a link in the long chain of signal beacons that linked Sabta (Ceuta) on the northern tip of Morocco with Alexandria in Egypt during Fatimid times. According to al-Maqrizi, some of these beacons were on stone towers standing next to the coast.

During the troubled 11th century, almost all Iranian cities were walled, including previously open cities. In most cases, however, it was a matter of refortifying the old urban centres and newly fortifying their suburbs. On other occasions the new suburb had become the main centre, sometimes because it was better fortified, while the old city declined. A further variation saw different quarters of a city being fortified while a new citadel was constructed on the edge of town. In general, however, these new Iranian fortifications tended to enclose substantially larger areas than the earlier defences. Nasir-i Khusraw described Shamiran (Samiran) in the mountains of north-western Iran as a castle with a triple wall and an underground canal to take drinking water from the river. It was, he said, garrisoned by 1,000 men plus their families. Much of Samiran has now been flooded by a man-made lake, but enough survives to show that Nasir-i Khusraw was a reliable observer.

THE LIVING SITES

During the Umayyad and early 'Abbasid caliphates, the appearance of fortification often seems to have been more important than the real strength. Both of those first ruling dynasties of caliphs inherited many of the 'imperial' attitudes of their Byzantine and Sassanian predecessors, even though such philosophies ran counter to the basic ethos of Islam. The deeply Iranian tradition of royal magnificence as a necessity of government eventually came to dominate many aspects of medieval Islamic statecraft. It had similarly been embedded within pre-Islamic Central Asian civilization, from which the Muslim Turks would draw so much of their 'ruling culture'. What would today be called conspicuous consumption became a means of expressing authority, and this included military architecture.

Though there was less separation between ruler and ruled during the Umayyad era, the fortified palace complex on Jabal al-Qal'a in the Jordanian capital of Amman was an early expression of this architectural trend. At its northern end were audience and throne rooms, plus four residential buildings, which were almost certainly home to a resident governor or relative of the ruling caliph. Umayyad court protocols were already beginning to follow those of the Sassanian *Shahinshah* emperors, where a ruler remained behind a curtain so that he was not visible to 'ordinary' people. It has therefore been suggested that a narrow passage between the audience rooms at Amman enabled the caliph to move around unseen. To one side of the entrance complex was a *hamam* bath-complex with its own cistern, similar to those of the preceding Hellenistic and Roman periods. In fact such *hamams* have been found in most Umayyad architectural complexes, and may have been another expression of privilege. A distinctly erotic bath scene also features prominently in the well preserved Umayyad wall-paintings at unfortified Qusayr 'Amra.

The 'Abbasid Caliphate saw this emphasis on display being taken to extreme length, and the Round City of Baghdad was largely designed as an arena for such political theatre. Here the Caliphal Palace and main mosque were located at the centre, within a huge open space that may have included parks, hunting or military training facilities. The other primary purpose of Baghdad and its surrounding suburbs was to accommodate large, diverse military forces at the centre of 'Abbasid power, with elite units such as the *haras* security forces and *shurta* police being housed in the second ring of the Round City itself. The regular army and lower grade paramilitary forces of the city garrison lived outside.

The 'Abbasid system was huge and impressive, but not without problems, and there were also significant military changes under way. Consequently, the moving of the 'Abbasid capital from the now huge metropolis of Baghdad to another newly founded city at Samarra was not merely a result of friction between soldiers and citizens. One of the main factors was a huge increase in the proportion of cavalry and the need for additional training areas, as well as newly irrigated land to grow their fodder.

Nor had the need to impress foreign visitors been forgotten. According to al-Khatib al-Baghdadi, the reception of Byzantine ambassadors at Samarra during the reign of the Caliph al-Muqtadir in the early 10th century AD involved military planning and the full use of monumental architecture as theatrical backdrops. The Byzantines apparently passed through different palaces on different days:

> [In the *al-Firdaws* Palace] was a corridor 300 cubits long, along the two sides of which were hung about 10,000 shields, helmets of leather, helmets of steel,

mail hauberks, ornamented quivers and bows… After they walked through 23 palaces [probably meaning rooms] they were led to the courtyard of the 90th Guards Regiment [so named because its men received 90 coins per month and were thus the highest paid in the caliph's army] where they found the *hujariyab* pages [youngsters under military training] assembled with their complete armament and best uniforms, offering a fine spectacle. They held in their hand crossbows, axes and maces.

The rival Fatimid Caliphate based in Egypt took the cult of mystery surrounding the person of the caliph even further. Like Baghdad and Samarra, al-Qahira (Cairo) was largely built of mud-brick, but this clearly did not detract from its magnificence. According to Nasir-i Khusraw, writing in AD 1047, the night garrison of Cairo consisted of 500 cavalry and 500 infantry to guard the palace. They also used trumpets, tambours and cymbals to announce the evening prayer, presumably as a supplement to the normal call to prayer from the minarets of the palace-city. Far to the east in Afghanistan, a description of a reception for envoys sent by the 'Abbasid caliph to Sultan Massud of Ghazna in AD 1031/2 shows that the traditional concern for spectacle remained strong. Here elite troops once again wore their finest costume and carried decorated weapons indicating their grades or status.

The fortifications on Jabal al-Qal'a, overlooking Amman, have been damaged by earthquakes and repaired several times. The relatively weak fortifications here, on the west side of the site, have buttresses or rudimentary towers that protrude only a short distance from the main wall. (Author's photograph)

The fortified cities

Magnificence was less of a concern for local or provincial authorities, or even for those defending a capital city. During the era of the first *Rashidun* ('Rightly Guided') and the Umayyad caliphs, one of the most important concerns for *walis* or provincial governors was the founding of new cities and maintaining or upgrading the fortifications of existing ones. Islamic rule was almost entirely based upon cities, and would to a large extent remain so throughout the medieval period.

One of the few large Arab garrisons in early Islamic Central Asia was at Marw, but elsewhere in the east troops seem to have been billeted in surrounding villages. Meanwhile, most cities here and in Iran soon consisted of almost autonomous, and frequently antagonistic, quarters. Another characteristic of such quarters was a tendency to spread along one of the main routes leading into a city. This could also be seen in the Middle East, and the names given to these quarters, especially if they consisted of suburbs outside an older walled city, often reflected local features, prominent structures and the original purpose or main trade of the quarter in question.

Other distinctively Islamic characteristics developed over the centuries both inside and outside urban fortifications. Some had a bearing upon the design of a particular city's defences and its armed forces. The *suq* or clearly defined market area was a case in point, not being seen earlier and not being present in the same form in other cultures. Such *suqs* were supervised by a *muhtasib*, an official recognized by the government whose responsibilities went beyond fair dealings, law and order within a market. He and his staff had a primary role in the supervision and location of buildings within a city, supervising design, building standards and the privacy required in Islamic domestic arrangements. On occasions he is even known to have had a say in the dimensions of mud bricks.

Another aspect of urban architecture that had a direct bearing upon defence were the pontoon bridges spanning major rivers, either within a city's fortified walls (as in Wasit) or next to them (as at Fustat, in the south of what

The new capital that the 'Abbasid caliph established at Samarra was not built around one fortified imperial palace as at Baghdad. Instead, several palace complexes were surrounded by walls, which often had a military appearance but a less real military function. They were, in fact, a form of political and military theatre. The Jawsaq al-Khaqani was built in AD 836 for the caliph al-Mu'tasim, overlooking the River Tigris. Its monumental, three-arched main entrance is the largest part still standing, and is known as the Bab al-'Amma. Behind it lay a magnificent throne room, the ruler's private quarters, a women's area or *harim*, a polo-ground, treasury and even a game preserve. In front lay a monumental stairway, a broad ornamental pool and lush gardens leading to the Tigris.

Top left inset: a plan of the Bab al-'Amma. The only true fortification element seems to have been the small rectangular tower a short distance to the left of the entrance stairs.

is now Cairo). At Fustat a pontoon bridge crossed the Nile in two stages via Geziret Island (*jazira* or 'island', with an Egyptian–Arabic accent) to what became the suburb of Giza (*jisr* or 'bridge', again with an Egyptian–Arabic accent). There were, of course, several such floating pontoon bridges across the Tigris in Baghdad.

The relatively high pay offered to professional soldiers throughout most of medieval Islamic civilization was another significant factor. It tended to be higher than the wages offered to workers and even skilled artisans, though one particularly well-paid group of soldiers in fact comprised military artisans. They formed the 'Abbasid army's corps of *manjaniqin* or siege machine operators and builders. In AD 744/5, during the reign of the Umayyad caliph Marwan II, there were 80 *manjaniq* stone-throwing machines in Hims alone. A century or so later, during the high point of 'Abbasid power and wealth, *manjaniqin* were stationed in all the main fortified cities and fortresses of the empire. At the other end of the military scale were *ahdath* urban militias who, despite being part-time volunteers, had clearly become significant political as well as military forces in regions like Syria and the Jazira.

The role of urban fortification differed from region to region, though it was always important, even in Arabia. In the mid-11th century, for example,

The four corner towers of the fortified city of Anjar are hollow, all the others being solid, and could be accessed at ground level from inside the fortifications. The wall of the tower consisted of an outer skin of large, well cut ashlar blocks and an inner skin of smaller but regularly cut stones, with the space between being filled with rubble. (Author's photograph)

Nasir-i Khusraw wrote that there were many strong fortresses in Najd in central Arabia, while Ta'if was a small town but had a well fortified castle. Further east, Yamamah, not far from the Gulf coast, was an old yet strong fortress and was the main town in an area that could field 400 horsemen. The town which Nasir-i Khusraw knew as Lahssa (in Arabic *al-Ahsa* between Yamamah and Basra) was another impressive fortress surrounded by four strong earth walls, and home to a substantial, warlike population.

Though there is no evidence of fortification in the main early medieval Egyptian city of Fustat, the ancestor of modern Cairo, one very specialized piece of military architecture did appear at the time of the first autonomous Tulunid ruler of Egypt, Ahmad Ibn Tulun (AD 868–84). It was a bridge or viaduct that ran from Fustat to the end of the pontoon bridge over the Nile. Consisting of 40 arches, it enabled an army to reach the bridge even when the annual Nile floods were at their height.

While medieval Egypt remained a land of villages with a few large towns and only a handful of cities, Syria had been one of the most urbanized parts of the world since ancient times. During the medieval period it remained a land of fortified cities, numerous strong castles and substantial garrisons. It also tended to be restless, not least under the Fatimid Caliphate, which never quite conquered Syria. The result was a complicated but well-recorded and largely urban military establishment. These Fatimid provincial garrisons were paid in a particular way, called *ijab mushahara*, which meant that the money came from the central army ministry of *diwan al-jaysh* each month, though it is unclear how much cash was actually moved around in bulk.

Precious little urban fortification survives from this tumultuous period, though it features prominently in written sources. Bakjur, one of the Fatimid governors of Syria, was said to have continued the construction of walls in Hims that had been started by his predecessors, but it is unclear whether these were around the city or were on the *tel* that served as a citadel. The ancient *tel* of Damascus formed a relatively low rise in the middle of the old city and was not a suitable position for a citadel. There was also a need to secure water supplies, the small and largely seasonal Barada River being linked to a system of irrigation canals between Damascus and Mount Qasyun to the north. The main irrigated territory of the Ghuta was, however, south of the city. Such neighbouring areas could provide additional fighting men, many of them being infantry archers in the old Syrian tradition. The cities also attracted settlers from surrounding rural communities and Bedouin tribes, though this was not a steady flow. In the late 10th century, for example, people flooded into Aleppo because invading Byzantine armies had devastated the countryside. The newcomers then provided useful troops, who were tough, capable of hard physical work and eager to hit back at their persecutors.

Iraq was generally less exposed to external invasion during this period, and its cities tended to be less troublesome to rulers. Wasit, for example, had been developed by the Umayyads as an expression of their dynastic power. Yet even Wasit was not entirely new since there was already a small pre-Islamic town on the eastern side of what was then the River Tigris. During the early Islamic period, Persians and Aramaean speakers lived in that old quarter, while Muslim Arabs settled in a newer, larger quarter established on the west bank of the river. The main Islamic monuments were also situated on the west bank until much later in the Middle Ages, including a governor's palace known as *al-Qubbat al-Khadra* because it had a green dome. It stood at some distance from the river and was 400 cubits square with four main entrances, which opened onto main streets that were 80 cubits wide. The main mosque was next door to the governor's palace, while the area towards the Tigris was a bazaar or commercial district. Next to the river itself was a large prison called the *Dimas*, which could reportedly accommodate thousands of people. North of this was a small harbour near the end of a pontoon bridge. The external gates of both halves of Wasit were closed at sunset after a formal summons for all strangers to leave the city.

At this time the River Tigris was navigable from the Persian Gulf to the town of Jazirat Ibn Umar, on what is now the south-eastern frontier of Turkey. It was so named because a wide curve in the river had been cut by a canal, supposedly credited to al-Hasan Ibn Umar. However, it was only briefly an artificial island, because the canal soon became the main course while the river's original course dried up. Jazirat Ibn Umar featured a bridge over the Tigris, was a major river port and was defended by an imposing mud-brick wall during the 10th century.

In Iran, the cities of Chalus on the Caspian coast of Tabaristan as well as Qazwin and Qum on the other side of the Elburz Mountains were all strongly defended against Daylami raiders from those mountains as early as the 8th century. Nasir-i Khusraw, who was normally a mine of information, merely stated that Isfahan had a crenellated wall with 'platforms' for soldiers.

Marw-i-Shahijan, or Great Marw, on the frontier of Khurasan and Central Asia was more than just a major garrison centre. It was a hub of long-distance trade, an industrial centre and the main city of an agricultural region whose irrigation system was controlled from the city itself. Here the Gavur-Qal'a had been the pre-Islamic Sassanian and early Islamic town while the Sultan-Qal'a immediately to the west developed from the 8th to 13th centuries, at which point it was destroyed by the Mongols. The remains of the wall built at a much greater distance from the centre of the city for the ancient Hellenistic Greek ruler Antiochus I were still visible in the 10th century and were sometimes called *al-Ray*. However, a breakdown in law, order and consequently in trade as the once powerful and wealthy Samanid dynasty declined led to a lack of maintenance of the mud-brick fortifications, and, according to al-Muqaddasi, both the city wall and citadel of Marw were in ruins by the 980s AD.

The great Central Asian city of Bukhara had a fortified outer wall during the Samanid period though it also became renowned for its crowded multi-storey buildings and a shortage of water because of its high location. Like Bukhara, Samarkand reached a height of wealth and splendour under Samamid rule in the 10th century. Within its massive earthen ramparts the houses were said to be of clay and wood, the former probably meaning unfired mud bricks. Drinking water was brought from the south to the central square by an aqueduct called the *ra's al-taq* in Arabic or *jun arziz* in Persian. This was a lead-lined, artificial channel or series of pipes, probably dating from

Boldumsay on the frontier of Uzbekistan and Turkmenistan had been fortified with mud-brick walls, towers and gates before the coming of Islam in the 8th century. These defences were maintained and perhaps strengthened until the catastrophic Mongol invasion of the 13th century, at which point the site was abandoned. (Author's photograph)

The south-eastern gate of Citadel of Harran was built, or rebuilt, in the 11th century with a horseshoe-arched entrance between solid, rectangular towers. Immediately over the doors was a carved stone inscription consisting of the single verse of Sura 112 of the *Koran*: 'Say, He is God alone, God the Eternal, He begets not and is not begotten. Nor is there like unto him any one.' This was an emphatic declaration of the basic difference between Islam and Christianity, rejecting the Christian belief in the divinity of Jesus Christ. The entire structure was faced with basalt, while the surrounds of the arched gate were decorated with basalt carvings, including pairs of hunting dogs on leashes (see inset). To the sides of the arch were carved birds, probably eagles with folded wings. Though the fragments are now too broken to be sure, this same motif was used in this same area a century later on Islamic metalwork. Another dedicatory inscription ran along the inwards facing walls of the towers and above the gate. It read: 'In the name of God the Merciful the Benevolent… [This is?] what has been ordered to be made, [by] our master, the Amir, the August Lord, whom God assists, the Victorious, Najib al-Dawla Radi al-Dawla Abu'l-Ziman son of the Amir Sani'at al-Dawla Safwat al-Dawla Abu'l-Rayyan Shabib son of Mu'ayyad al-Dawla Waththab son of Ja'bar the Numayrid in the year 451'. The Numayrid ruler in question is more commonly known as Mani Ibn Shabib, who dominated Harran from AD 1040 until 1063, while the Islamic date of 451 AH ran from 17 February AD 1059 until 6 February AD 1060.

pre-Islamic times, but which was maintained by Samarkand's Zoroastrian inhabitants in return for tax exemptions. It was also used to irrigate extensive gardens within the city and to fill various ornamental pools.

The cities of the upland valley of Farghana had expanded outside their ancient defences in the prosperous period immediately before the Islamic conquest. The early period of indirect Arab rule in the 8th and 9th centuries then saw the development of a fragmented feudalism followed by a further increase of urbanism and prosperity through trade along the Silk Roads. This continued into the 12th century, when conquest by the non-Islamic, largely Buddhist Qara Khitai was followed by an even more devastating Mongol onslaught. During this early medieval period, the towns of Farghana were characteristically divided into an *ark* or *kukhendiz* citadel containing the ruler's palace, a *shakhristan* (or in Arabic the *madina*) inner city and *rabid* suburbs where most crafts and trades were located. One such city was Kuva, the second city of the Farghana Valley after Akhiset. Described as well watered and green, it had a citadel which covered 12 hectares, plus *rabid* suburbs to the east, west and south covering one and a half square kilometres. It is also worth noting that Buddhism survived in Kuva well beyond the 8th-century Islamic conquest, with a Buddhist temple being erected even in the 12th or 13th century – though this might reflect a revival of Buddhism following the Qara Khitai conquest.

A lot is known about life along this Central Asian frontier. Here, the 10th-century Arab geographer Ibn Hawqal described Uzgend as:

> the last city of Farghana adjoining the land of the *kafirs* [non-Muslim pagans].
> It is as large as two thirds of Osh. It has a citadel, fortified *shakhristan* and
> *rabid*, with bazaars located therein. Uzgend is a trading centre at the borderline
> with the land of the Turks. Gardens and canals are laid around the city.

Al-Muqaddasi's description was more detailed:

> There is a river at the gates of Uzgend that one should cross by fording, as
> there are no bridges across. The suburbs of the city are surrounded by walls.
> The city centre is densely populated, there are bazaars, a congregational
> mosque [the main mosque used for public prayers on Fridays] and a citadel.
> Water goes to every citizen. The city has four gates. I doubt if there are any
> other cities in the region which have a citadel superior to that of Uzgend.

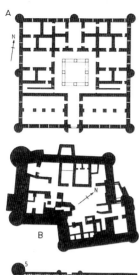

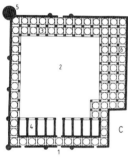

Commercial and pilgrim fortifications.
A: Qasr al-Kharana, Umayyad so-called 'desert palace' standing at junction of five traditional desert routes and dating from before AD 710. Some internal stabling appears to have been for camels (after S. Urice).
B: one of several fortified buildings at al-Rabadhah, Saudi Arabia, on the Darb al-Zubaydah pilgrim road between Iraq and Mecca, late 8th to early 10th centuries AD (after S. Ibn Abd al-Aziz al-Rashid).
C: caravanserai at Kishman-tepe (Kushmeihan), Turkmenistan – one of the earliest fortified way-stations on the 'Silk Roads' across Central Asia, 9th century AD (after G.A. Federov-Davydov). 1 – main entrance; 2 – central courtyard for loading and unloading; 3 – domed storage areas; 4 – *hujra*, accommodation cells; 5 – single defensive tower.

Archaeological research confirms that medieval Uzgend was much bigger than the modern town, occupying much of the area between the Jassy and Kara-Darya rivers, its central part consisting of four distinct *shakhristans* on the right bank of the Kara-Darya.

The clearest description of nearby Osh comes from al-Istakhri, writing in the 10th century:

> This is a lively city surrounded by walls. There are a citadel and an amir's palace. The city adjoins the mountains where there is a guard post to watch the Turks [today this guardpost is marked by a small but not particularly old Islamic shrine]… Osh matches Kuva in size. The *shakhristan* and *kukhendiz* are provided with amenities, both the amir's palace and the jail are within the *kukhendiz*. The *rabid* is in the *shakhristan*. The *rabid* is surrounded by walls and the wall reaches the mountain where the guards are watching the Turkish troops [largely still pagan at that date]. There are three gates in Osh; the Darvaza-i Kukh, the Darvaza-i Ab and the Darvaza-i Mugkede.

THE SITES AT WAR

Offensive bases

The highly mobile, multiple approach and strategically offensive philosophy of medieval Islamic warfare limited the importance of minor fortifications. In fact the only military sites that played a significant role in such warfare were the fortified cities.

After the Muslim Arabs conquered Syria, Byzantine forces retreated into Anatolia, abandoned the Cilician towns east of the Ceyhan River and laid waste to the entire region they could not defend. However, this neither halted nor slowed the Islamic advance, and the Arabs easily conquered all of Cilicia, including Adana and the low-lying coastal plain. Throughout the Umayyad period Cilicia remained a no-man's land, nominally Islamic, but not refortified except for Massisah (Misis) on the Ceyhan River, which served as a forward base.

After a pause while the Umayyad Caliphate was rent by civil war and overthrown by the 'Abbasids, who then suffered their own decades of civil war, serious raiding into Byzantine territory revived in the late 8th century. Some were launched in winter, but it was not until the turn of 8th/9th century that the caliphs decided to repopulate Cilicia, repair its fortifications and construct new garrison forts. Thereafter the fortified cities of Cilicia served as bases from which almost annual raids were sent across the Taurus Mountains, deep into Byzantine territory.

Unfortunately, Arabic chronicles did not always distinguish between substantial field fortifications and permanent works. Hence, it is not always clear what sort of defences were erected even in major Iraqi campaigns like those of Caliph Mu'tasim's reign in the first half of the 9th century. These were wide-ranging campaigns, although they were carefully planned, cautious, often slow-moving and faced different foes in very different geographical circumstances. Great effort was focused on securing an army's communications, both against rebels led by Babik in the mountainous north of Iraq and against the *Zutt* or *Zanj* rebels in the southern marshlands.

It is also worth noting that Mu'tasim put a general named Afshin in command against Babik because he came from Central Asia and had experience of mountain warfare. In fact Afshin used new tactics, and instead of the sudden raids by expeditionary forces that had characterized previous Islamic campaigns, he advanced slowly with a notably large army, taking territory and consolidating his hold by building fortifications. Afshin also sent out numerous reconnaissance forces and secured the rear areas, while the caliph supported this campaign with regular supplies and reinforcements. Though Afshin's army included many linguistic and cultural groups, the primary role of the elite Turkish *ghulam* or *mamluk* units was to protect supply lines and hold fortified positions.

The campaign against the *Zutt* in southern Iraq involved comparable strategy. Here Mu'tasim's army was commanded by Ujaif Ibn Anbasa, a veteran Arab general who sealed all the river outlets from the marshes to stop fleets of enemy raiders. This may have involved semi-permanent fortifications. Ibn Anbasa's army next made the same careful, steady and consolidated advance as Afshin undertook in the north, with the protection of communications and supply lines as a primary consideration.

The same limited use of fortifications as offensive bases continued almost unchanged until the later 11th century, when the arrival of the Seljuk Turks and the Western European Crusaders exposed the limitations of such strategy. However, naval campaigns always depended upon secure home bases. Thus the vital strategic importance of the fleet to the Fatimid Caliphate of Egypt and Syria meant a corresponding emphasis on coastal fortifications. Indeed, the Fatimids' tenuous hold upon Syria relied upon their ability to send reinforcements and supplies by sea from Egypt.

Fortifications of Central Asia. A–B: Tower 2 of the second *shahristan* or citadel of Baykand (Paikend) in Uzbekistan, pre-Islamic but remaining in use until the 9th century AD (after A.R. Mukhamedkhanov et al.). A – isometric reconstruction; B – plan of upper floor. C: isometric reconstruction of a section of the brick citadel of Balkh, Afghanistan, in the 7th and 8th centuries AD (after E. Esin).

Castles under siege

One of the first military efforts by the Prophet Muhammad and his followers was against some of the tall, fortified houses that characterized Arabian oases. Those at Khaybar contained siege engines, which could be used against the fortified houses or 'castles' of rivals during civil conflict. The machines in question appear to have been *'arrada* – simple, small forms of man-powered, beam-sling mangonels – while one fortified house captured by the Muslims also contained two roofed wooden 'sheds' to protect miners as they attacked the base of an enemy wall.

Accounts of siege warfare in the Umayyad period indicate that some fortifications in the Islamic heartlands were not particularly effective. For example, when the Umayyad caliph Walid II decided against seeking refuge in the Syrian desert city of Palmyra because its population was unreliable, he retreated to the *qasr* of al-Bakhra which was a day's march away. It consisted of a rectangular fort described as *hasin*, meaning well fortified, which had been built by *'ajam* or 'foreigners' – in this case Romans. It had 'boldly projecting hollow towers' and can probably be identified as Khan al-Hallabat (Roman Veriaraca). Even though al-Walid II's pursuers had no siege engines, they scaled the walls to take al-Bakhra with ease.

THE REPAIRING OF HARUNIYE CASTLE, AD 967

Several features in the existing castle of Haruniye are so advanced that they are unlikely to date from its foundation by the caliph Harun al-Rashid in the late 8th century. This is probably true of the covered gallery, with its large and sophisticated embrasures that defend the most vulnerable side of the castle. They are most likely to date from the 10th century, perhaps from the extensive repairs that were carried out following a Byzantine attempt to destroy Haruniye. The interiors of these stirrup-shaped embrasures were very deep and broad, perhaps to provide space for large crossbows of a type known to have been used to defend fortifications during this period. An upper wall-walk was accessed by stairs inside the castle and a passage within the wall. The only

remaining openings for a lost upper level are two narrow, embrasured windows, both covered by pointed arches and with sills that are steeply angled to aid observation or enable an archer to shoot downwards. Outside the castle there had been a small walled town with 1,500 inhabitants, who were abducted by a Byzantine army in AD 959. Sayf al-Dawla's engineers, architects and craftsmen also repaired this town as well as the castle.

Inset: plan of Haruniye, late 10th century, showing the defences concentrated along one side. A – south-western gate; B – smaller defensive gallery; C – larger defensive gallery; D – north-eastern gate; E – great tower; F – small vaulted room; G – only embrasure facing south or east.

Siege warfare became more serious during the 'Abbasid period, and this almost certainly lay behind the rising importance of crossbows of various sizes, and eventually of counterweight forms of stone-throwing mangonel. A remarkable 9th-century 'Abbasid military manual by al-Harthami, the earliest version of which survives as a Fatimid abbreviation, included an entire section on offensive warfare. Chapter 13 concerned 'Fortification near the place of departure and during the journey', largely covering field fortifications, while chapter 15 concerned 'Fortified camps and the place of arrival'. However, chapter 34 focused on offensive siege warfare against substantial fortifications and the defence of the besieger's camps, while chapter 35 focused on the defence of such fortifications. The manual lists required equipment, and then advises a commander to:

identify positions for laying down crossing points and fords and bridges [of various types], to identify positions for erecting the *manjaniq* and *'arradat* [large and small forms of man-powered mangonels] and identify [select or have made] their stones and decide what to damage [identify their targets], identify the positions for archers using *nishab* [heavy] arrows, and 'snakes' [unclear] and stone quarries [for mangonel missiles], identify the position for the *'ijl* [literally 'calf', perhaps a device to batter walls or gates] and rams and openings [as weak points in the wall] and slopes [easy points of approach] and encourage work against it, identify the positions for the ladders and the hooks and the 'snatching away' and the 'plucking' [meaning the demolition of the walls]. Hurry to erect the *manjaniqs* that do the work.

The fortress at Ayn Umm al-Dabaqi, in the south-western Egyptian desert, stood near the northern stretch of the Darb al-Arbain 'Forty Days Road' from Nubia and Darfur in the Sudan. One raid by Christian Nubian forces carried off a large part of the population of the Western Oases in the AD 950s. (Author's photograph)

Collapsed
Moat

The huge Persian *Shahnamah* epic by Firdawsi, written around 1000 AD, describes many open battles between vast armies. However, sieges are sometimes described in detail, as in the following passage:

Thus he disposed his
forces and, resuming
His seat upon the throne,
required the troops
To excavate
entrenchments round
the fortress
Then all who had
experience in sieges
From Rum [Byzantium],
China, India, with
veteran chiefs
From every quarter,
rode around the place
Like couriers, devising
plans to take it
The monarch made
a trench two spears
in depth
And stationed guards
that none might make
a sally
By night and slay his
troops ere they could
draw
Around were arrayed
two hundred *arbalists*
[*charkh* crossbow
operators]
And when a foe's head
showed above the
ramparts
These engines showered
like hail there; behind
Were Ruman [Byzantium]
troops engaged in
working them
The Shah then bade that
elephants should draw
Shores [props] to the
hold. He undermined
the walls
And shored them up;
upon the wooden
props
He smeared black
naptha [incendiary
naft], such was his
device
Whereby the walls were
stayed and
overthrown.

(Firdawsi, Abu'l-Qasim
(tr. A.G. Warner and E. Warner),
The Shahnama of Firdausi
(London, 1905), 208;
and Firdawsi, Abu'l-Qasim
(ed. J.A. Vullers), *Shahname*
(Leiden, 1877–80), 1333–39)

Another paragraph advised the commander of a fortified place facing a siege to:

Remove from the materials [in the castle] that which is rotten and outdated and not longer useful… Do not remove equipment from the parts of the castle which need to be strong such as gates and *arkan* [corners] and towers and *shuraf* [battlements] and *suturah* [screens] and doors and the *muharis* [guard posts] and the *manazir* [watchtowers].

The intensive castle-warfare of the 10th and 11th centuries in south-eastern Anatolia and northern Syria featured prominently in documents from the period. The mountain passes used by Umayyad and 'Abbasid raiders in earlier years were still used by Byzantine invaders and in Hamdanid Arab attempts at retaliation – the same fortresses also being mentioned again and again. Some of the most detailed accounts of siege warfare in this period are found in Arabic poems written at the court of Sayf al-Dawla. They mention siege machines that hurled *naft*, or Greek Fire – such advanced military technology now being available throughout the Middle East. In the 10th and 11th centuries even Bedouin Arab tribal forces used stone-throwing *manjaniq* mangonels when attacking enemy fortifications, though the wealthy and powerful Byzantine Empire could do this on a much larger scale.

Cities under siege and civil conflict

The famous Battle of the Ditch, or *al-Khandaq*, featured prominently in Islamic accounts of the life of the Prophet Muhammad. According to generally accepted accounts, the idea for defending Medina with a ditch or moat came from one of the Prophet's first non-Arab adherents, Salman the Persian, and was therefore regarded as a new and almost un-Arab method of fighting. Nevertheless, it was accepted by the Prophet and the ditch was excavated in six days, close enough to the town for the outermost houses to serve as strongpoints, from whose roofs missiles could be hurled at the attackers. The ditch itself cut across the valley floor between rocky hillsides and was intended as a barrier against cavalry assault.

Muhammad's followers successfully defended Medina, but failed when they themselves attacked the fortified town of Ta'if, south of Mecca. At the time Ta'if was well fortified with strong gates, and guarded by archers. More importantly, the town was well provisioned and the defenders had brought in Yemenis who knew how to make and operate *manjaniqs* that could hurl 'red hot metal' against the attackers' siege devices. Only half a century later Mecca itself was besieged in a civil war that threatened to tear the new Islamic state apart. By now the numbers and effectiveness of the siege machines had increased so that these *manjaniqs* could hurl incendiary material right into the city.

In AD 684, Arab troops of the Bakri tribe that had settled in Khurasan rose in revolt against the Umayyad governor of Harat. Their leader Aws Ibn Tha'laba advised them to remain inside their well-fortified town, but the Bakris insisted on facing the enemy outside it, where they excavated a *khandaq* anti-cavalry ditch. In fact there seems to have been a continuing belief that remaining behind walls limited an army's options. When real sieges did take place, they tended to be resolved by negotiation rather than direct attack. Sometimes a direct assault did occur. In AD 704, a joint army of Tibetans, Turks and *Hayatilah* (Hephthalites descended from the Huns) breached the walls of Muslim-held Tirmidh (Termez) in southern Uzbekistan. However, they were defeated by a sortie of heavily armoured Muslim cavalry.

One of the largest urban sieges of this period was the 'Abbasid attack on Wasit in AD 749. Both parts of the city, on each bank of the Tigris, were garrisoned by Umayyad troops, which included the elite *Ahl al-Sham* 'People of Syria' and were led by a highly experienced commander named Yazid Ibn Hubayra. The 'Abbasid army had already captured Kufa and so attacked Wasit from the west, making camp facing the *Bab al-Midmar* (the unidentified 'Racetrack Gate' which probably lay in the western section of Wasit). As usual, the struggle began with sorties by the Umayyad defenders, but these were forced back to the moat that defended the walls. Some Umayyad cavalry were said to have been pushed to the edge of the river, where some escaped in boats sent from the city while others drowned.

The siege of Wasit dragged on for a year, during which the defenders bombarded their foes with mangonel stones from inside the city. On the river the 'Abbasids tried to destroy a pontoon bridge that connected Wasit's two parts. However, men in small boats used hooks to pull these fireships away. There was also considerable nightfighting along the wall and towers that lined the inside of the moat; here the defenders erected torches so that they could shoot at the attackers. Meanwhile the brave, old Umayyad commander observed events from a *burj* or tower above the Bab al-Khallalin gate. Eventually the Umayyad army crumbled, and the last to resist were described as *fityan* and *sa'alik*, perhaps best translated as regular soldiers loyal to Ibn Hubayra and mercenaries or 'ruffians' from the city itself.

The 'Abbasid period witnessed many civil wars, some of which almost tore the empire apart. In AD 812, during the struggle between Harun al-Rashid's sons, the current caliph al-Amin and his brother the future caliph al-Mamun, the city of Ruha (Urfa) nearly fell to rebels. So the caliph insisted that it be strongly fortified, though the citizens had to pay for these defences themselves. The biggest sieges of these war-torn years were those of Baghdad itself. In AD 812/3 the 'Abbasid capital was held by al-Amin and was attacked by Tahir 'the Ambidextrous' on behalf of al-Mamun. During this prolonged siege, Tahir's artillerymen set up stone-throwing weapons along the River Tigris to stop supply ships getting through. There was also bitter street-fighting, but after al-Amin was forced to retreat into the Round City the latter only resisted for one day because the supply of drinking water was inadequate.

Abu Amr Uthman al-Tarsusi's account of the methods used to defend the frontier city of Tarsus in the 10th century are astonishingly detailed, as when the *ghazis*, or religiously motivated volunteers, were called to arms:

> The person who is in charge of the functions of *hisba* [public organization], at whatever time the summons to arms may occur, whether at night or in the daytime, rides forth with his foot soldiers before him. They shout in unison, at the tops of their voices, 'To arms, O cavalrymen and infantrymen, to arms – may God provide you with the due stimulus – at the Bab al-Jihad!' And if he wishes them to rally at the Bab Qatamiyya, at the Bab al-Saff, or at any other gate there may be, he locks the rest of the gates of the *madina* [inner city] and their keys are left with the *sahib al-shurta* [chief of police]. The gates remain locked until the representative of the Sultan returns from the summons to arms and takes up his residence again in his palace. All the locked gates are then opened, and the *muhtasib* [officer in charge of *hisba*] and his staff of foot soldiers go round all the main streets and highways. If all that takes place during the daytime, a considerable number of *sibyan* [boys, youths] are added to the *muhtasib's* staff of foot soldiers, and these *sibyan* assist the latter in proclaiming

For epic poetic accounts of sieges in the late 10th century, the Persian *Shahnamah* can hardly be bettered. One of its descriptions concerns the preparations made by Afrasiab, the Turkish ruler of Central Asia:

> Afrasiayab for his part,
>   at Gang [now the
>   southernmost part
>   of Turkmenistan]
> Abandoned quiet
>   banqueting, and sleep
> Arranged his catapults
>   ['*arrada*] upon the
>   walls
> And fitted up the towers
>   to stand a siege
> He bade magicians *myri*
>   bring up mighty stones
> Upon the walls, he
>   summoned many
>   experts
> From Rum [Byzantium],
>   and stationed troops
>   upon the ramparts
> A *prelatae*, shrewd of
>   heart, set up thereon
> Ballistas ['*arrada*]
>   catapults [*manjaniq*]
>   and arbalists [*charkh*
>   crossbows]
> And shields of wolf-hide.
>   All the towers were
>   filled
> With coats of mail and
>   helms. He kept a troop
> Of smiths at work to
>   fashion claws of steel
> On every side and bind
>   them to long spears
> To grapple any that
>   ventured nigh
> Or, if not that, to make
>   him shun the hold
> In all his dealings he was
>   just, he gave
> His troops their pay and
>   well entreated them
> He gave moreover helms
>   and scimitars
>   [*shamshir*]
> Mail for the chargers
>   [*bargustuwan*
>   horse-armour], shields
>   from Chin, with bows
> And arrows to his men
>   past reckoning.

(Firdawsi, Abu'l-Qasim (tr. A.G. Warner and E. Warner), *The Shahnama of Firdausi* (London, 1905), 197; and Firdawsi, Abu'l-Qasim (ed. J.A. Vullers), *Shahname* (Leiden, 1877–80), 1327–28)

53

The surrender of Bunjikath to the Muslim Karakhanids by its Samanid garrison was a significant event, the year AD 999 being a turning point in Central Asian history. It marked the fall of the essentially Iranian Samanids and the shifting of political and cultural domination to the Turks, of whom the Karakhanid dynasty were the first truly Islamic dynasty. The Qala'i-i Kahkakha itself was a small citadel attached to the curtain wall of the fortified Central Asian city of Bunjikath. Its lower part was made of large stone blocks forming a sloping plinth or talus, while the stone wall above was integral with the circuit-wall of the town. The upper part of the citadel was constructed of brick covered with stucco plaster and topped by a row of crenellations. Lower right inset: a section through the castle from the city wall on the right, indicated by a different colour to the inner wall on the left. The main internal entrance chamber was illuminated by a light-well in a roof which was supported by wooden pillars. An upper chamber facing the town was similarly illuminated through the roof.

the call to arms. Sometimes a general *hashad* [muster] of the populace has to be resorted to when matters become serious and the situation difficult. In that case the *muhtasib* orders all the market traders to come to arms and urges them the go forth behind the *Amir* [commander], whatever way he takes and however he travels.[5]

When Tarsus eventually surrendered to the Byzantine army this was done by negotiation and there was no massacre, though the Muslim population was expelled. In contrast, when the Byzantines captured Ayn Zarba in AD 962 they slaughtered men, women, children and babies. They then cut down 50,000 palm trees and expelled the surviving inhabitants, most of whom died on the roads as they tried to find refuge elsewhere. Finally, the Byzantine army demolished the entire city and its fortifications. That same year a Byzantine army managed to take the city of Aleppo, deporting many inhabitants to Byzantine territory, though other citizens and the defending garrison held out in the citadel hill. There were few if any fortifications on the hill at that date, so the defenders built barricades made of donkey and horse saddles.

The Arab–Islamic states of the Middle East were still under pressure from the Byzantine Empire during the first half of the 11th century. They were also involved in bitter inter-Islamic struggles that often pitted Sunni against Shi'a. Though some of the resulting warfare was small-scale and localized, it also often involved fortifications that might be demolished merely for posing a perceived threat. This was the fate of three small castles near Aleppo in 1002, when the governor of Aleppo felt that their mere existence threatened his position.

Aleppo itself would be at the centre of local conflicts for the rest of the century, after which it became one of the first centres of resistance to the Crusader threat. During one civil war in Aleppo in AD 1024, a large house near the citadel-hill was used as an urban fortress by the pro-Fatimid faction. This strongpoint was then attacked by the rival faction, both sides using stone-throwing *manjaniqs* and *jarradat* (large shields or mantlets). The attackers now dug a mine towards the house, burned the props and caused a wall to collapse. Large crossbows were meanwhile used by a Fatimid garrison on the citadel hill in an effort to support those men

The fortifications of Qasr al-Hayr al-Gharbi in Syria were largely symbolic, being covered in elaborately carved and flimsy stucco panels, columns and arches. However, this flimsiness enabled archaeologists to transport and reassemble the shattered fragments outside the main entrance to the National Museum in Damascus. (Author's photograph)

5 C.E. Bosworth, 'Abu 'Amr 'Uthman al-Tarsusi's *Siyar al Thughur* and the Last Years of Arab Rule in Tarsus (Fourth/Tenth Century)', *Graeco-Arabica*, 5 (1993), 191–92.

G

The eastern gate of the Umayyad fortified city of Anjar in Lebanon's fertile Baqa'a Valley. Beyond was a shop-lined street with the main mosque and large palace on the left, and a smaller palace on the right. (Author's photograph)

One of the most distinctive features of the castle of Haruniye, north of Antioch in Turkey, is a decorative use of rows of almost black basalt and almost white limestone. Those seen here flank the collapsed north-eastern gate. (Author's photograph)

defending the fortified house below. By now there was clearly some form of fortification on the hill, because the attackers next besieged the citadel itself, excavating a mine, which penetrated the well shaft or cistern that supplied the defenders with drinking water. This enabled them to cut the ropes of the defenders' water buckets and to fill the well with rocks.

Eighteen years later Aleppo was convulsed by further disturbances, descriptions of which show that the city wall had linked up with that of the citadel near the eastern gate. The Fatimid struggle to control Syria involved many urban sieges, several of them focussed upon Damascus, and these events were remarkably well documented. Different systems of summoning soldiers and militias were reported. Whereas in 10th-century Cairo this was done by public criers in the *suq* marketplaces who called the men to designated places where they would receive their arms and armour, this was probably not the method used in a sudden emergency. In Damascus, the *nafir* 'alarm' sounded when an enemy attacked, whereupon armed men rushed to man the walls and towers; this was probably the normal method when an assault was launched during an otherwise prolonged siege. Those who responded clearly included the *ahdath* urban militias, who were sometimes simply described as the 'young men' of the city.

During one such attack upon Damascus by Fatimid *Maghribi* 'North African' troops in October AD 970, the city's militia tried to face the enemy outside their fortifications, in a manner often described in earlier centuries. But their array was broken and the men retreated inside the walls, whereupon their commander had the city gates closed and archers stationed along the curtain wall to shoot at the North Africans from behind the crenellations. On other occasions it is clear that the archers were concentrated above the city gates. The defenders of Damascus also used slings during the 10th century, sacks of the sling-stones being brought to the men by donkeys. A reference to simple *'arrada* forms of man-powered, stone-throwing mangonels being mounted on the walls in AD 983 was not the only example of such practice. That same year they were used against Fatimid troops who were approaching the fortifications, but the mangonel operators were opposed by the Fatimids' numerous archers, probably recruited in what is now Jordan and Palestine, who kept the defenders' heads down.

A further interesting feature of sieges of Damascus during the 10th and 11th centuries was the importance of the *Ghuta*, or irrigated and densely cultivated oasis, which almost surrounded the city. Some of its groves of walnut trees grew so close to the city that they were used by the defenders to ambush isolated or small units of enemy cavalry and infantry. In fact, the only large open spaces immediately outside Damascus were the *maydans*, cavalry training grounds, which were used by market stallholders and craftsmen when not required by the military.

The *Ghuta* itself was, and still is, dotted with villages, with gardens walled with mud brick or stone – today usually by breezeblocks. Its numerous irrigation ditches were crossed by flimsy wooden bridges and the whole area posed a major problem for besieging armies. The terraces of big country houses in the *Ghuta* were similarly used as strongpoints from which to harass the enemy. There was often close cooperation between the city and the *Ghuta* villages during this period, and streetfighting in the suburbs close to the city walls was a common feature of such sieges. Not surprisingly, the *ahdath* or city militia of Damascus proved themselves highly effective in such circumstances because of their close knowledge of the terrain.

All sides used *naft* or 'Greek Fire' incendiary weapons during this period, and this could prove devastating against country houses serving as military positions in the *Ghuta*. Nevertheless, the independent spirit and warlike character of the people of Damascus remained a problem for the Fatimid Caliphate. On at least one occasion a Fatimid commander and governor had breaks knocked through the circuit wall, as well as taking the gates off their hinges, to strengthen his hold on the city. He then installed a garrison in houses across Damascus. Perhaps partly as a result of the aggressive spirit of Syrian cities and out of concern that relieving forces might arrive from elsewhere, attackers sometimes placed their base camps a long way from the city walls. When Jawhar besieged Damascus in AD 976, for example, he built a camp surrounded by a ditch and garrisoned with a substantial force south-west of the city, between Shamma'iyya and Daraya to the control roads from what are now northern Jordan and northern Palestine. A few years earlier another Fatimid commander named Ja'far besieged Tiberius. As part of this operation he constructed a fortress to control a bridge over the River Jordan between al-Sinabra and Fiq on the Golan Heights.

AFTERMATH

The second half of the 11th century saw the beginning of major changes in the eastern and central Islamic lands. The Seljuk Turks continued their advance from Central Asia, across Iran to take control of virtually the entire Fertile Crescent. They drove the Byzantine Empire back far beyond the frontiers that had lasted from the late 7th to the early 10th century, and in the process triggered the Crusades. Meanwhile, longer-established Turkish dynasties in

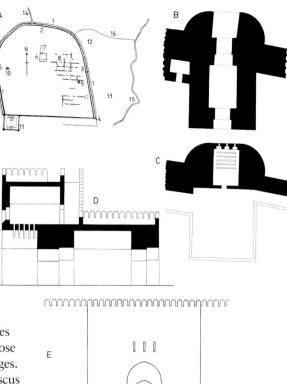

A: the fortified half-round city of al-Rafiqa (Raqqa), founded by the caliph al-Mansur around AD 772, soon surrounded by additional suburbs and palace complexes, most of which remained unfortified (after N. Hagen et al.). 1 – fortified wall surrounding al-Rafiqa, with a moat all around except outside the southern wall overlooking the Euphrates River; 2 – north gate; 3 – Bab al-Sibal, east gate; 4 – Bab Baghdad, south-eastern gate; 5 – west gate; 6 – main mosque; 7 – cistern; 8 – surviving grid pattern of streets; 9 – Qasr al-Banat small palace; 10 – main palace of the caliph Harun al-Rashid; 11 – 'Ayyubid citadel, late 12th or early 13th century; 12 – suburb of 9th or 10th century; 13 – suburb of al-Raqqa al-Muhtariqa; 14–15 – irrigation and drainage canals; 16 – defensive wall built by Tahir Ibn al-Husayn.
B–E: north gate of al-Rafiqa (after N. Hagen et al.). B – ground plan. C – plan of upper chamber. D – restored section through gate. E – restored elevation of gate viewed from outside the fortifications.

Afghanistan spread Islamic control deeper into northern India. The Fatimid Caliphate survived in Egypt and parts of the Syro-Palestinian coast, remaining the only major Middle Eastern Islamic state from the pre-Turkish era. Then came the First Crusade and the establishment of Crusader States in the Middle East at the close of the 11th century.

Some of the finest surviving examples of early medieval Islamic fortification date from the latter part of the 11th century, most notably the late Fatimid gates of Cairo, which were intended to face an anticipated Turkish rather than the unexpected Crusader assault. They have been said to reflect Armenian architectural influence, and Armenians undoubtedly played a significant military role in the later Fatimid state, not least under a number of Armenian army commanders and chief *wazirs*, or 'first ministers'.

The number and sophistication of fortifications in Syria similarly increased, partly because of the Fatimid Caliphate's inability to pacify the country. As a result, each area was protected by a garrison about a day's march apart, often owing only nominal allegiance to the Fatimids, while the strongly fortified coastal cities became virtually independent of both the declining Fatimids and the rising Seljuk Turks. In fact, 12 of the 14 walled cities that fell under Crusader control had been fortified before they arrived. Society in many such cities was now distinctly war-orientated, and in Edessa (Urfa), for example, many inhabitants kept arms and armour in their own homes. Urban militias of the *ahdath* type were similarly widespread and effective.

Despite numerous invasions, liberations and changes of regime across the Middle East and Central Asia in the following centuries, there would also be remarkable continuity, especially in terms of military architecture. Brick fortification continued to be built in the Euphrates region of eastern Syria well into the 12th century. On the other hand, the idea that the ancient city wall of Damascus survived 'virtually unchanged' into the 20th century is nonsense. Most of the present wall follows a curved line, and although the bases of some finely built towers can be seen beneath later and cruder masonry, many appear to be medieval rather than Roman. Furthermore, the early medieval wall of Damascus was at least partially built of mud brick, when all the existing wall is stone.

Archaeological excavation shows that some Umayyad fortifications continued to be inhabited. For example, there appears to have been a 14th-century Mamluk garrison in the small enclosure of Qasr al-Hayr al-Sharqi. The walls of Tinnis on Egypt's delta coast were strengthened and a citadel built for Saladin in AD 1181/2, but only a decade later the overwhelming naval superiority of the Western European fleets led to the abandonment of the town, although a garrison remained.

Far to the north-east, the fortified Sultan Qal'a of Marw was rebuilt for the Great Seljuk sultan Malik Shah between AD 1070 and 1080, and its ruins remain impressive to this day. This cannot be said of the gates of Kuva in the Farghana Valley. They were rebuilt in the 11th–12th century, one at least being reduced from 4.5m to 2.2m wide. Perhaps a new, and as yet undiscovered, gate was built, while this example was converted into a military postern. The fortified *shakhristan* of Kuva was similarly strengthened, though still with *pakhsa* and bricks; it remained in use until the entire region was devastated by the Mongols in the early 13th century.

Although the golden age of Islamic science and technology is often said to have ended in the 11th century, the process of development did not cease. The biggest single impetus to change in military architecture was the widespread adoption of increasingly powerful and accurate counterweight beam-sling mangonels. This began early in the Ayyubid 13th century and resulted in massive towers that served as artillery bastions, as well as more massive walls to resist the attackers' mangonels.

The eastern Islamic regions saw their biggest changes in the aftermath of the Mongol invasions, which were followed by a notable spread of Chinese artistic and technological influence. However, this had a minimal impact upon Islamic architecture, and surprisingly little upon fortification. The city of Bam in south-eastern Iran continued to flourish because of its position on a spur of the network of roads linking the Middle East and China. It eventually covered some six square kilometres, surrounded by a rampart with 38 towers and dominated by a brick citadel. Sadly, Bam and its medieval fortifications were almost totally destroyed by earthquake in 2003. Finally, it is important to remember that there were equally splendid fortified cities beyond the medieval Islamic frontier in *kafir* (non-Islamic) Central Asia during this period, especially in the mountains and along the Silk Roads. These included sometimes fortified religious buildings, of which the Buddhist examples appear to have been especially fine. In this context the idea of supposedly primitive Mongols suddenly erupting from nowhere is clearly only part of the story.

THE SITES TODAY

Any account at what can now be seen of the early medieval Islamic fortifications described in this book must start from the point that two of the most important regions are currently 'off-limits' for the normal traveller, namely Iraq and Afghanistan. Fortifications in the Kurdish regions of south-eastern Turkey are hardly much easier to visit at the time of writing, though the basic tourist and transport facilities are still in place.

Meanwhile, neighbouring Iran is much easier to visit and to explore than certain governments would have us believe. Fortunately, the main Umayyad fortifications, real and perhaps symbolic, are found in Syria, Jordan and Lebanon, the first two of which are certainly more accessible, though Lebanon is a little more tense. Libya is opening up to visitors at a remarkable rate, while Egypt poses few problems. At present there is almost nothing to see at Tinnis except a few bumps in the surface of the island. The castle at 'Ayn Umm al-Dabaqi and its tiny, surrounding, deserted oasis, is both expensive and difficult to reach, with even four-wheel-drive vehicles getting stuck in the surrounding sand dunes.

Afghanistan
Lashkari Bazar: part of the largely 12th–13th-century southern castle might date from the 11th century.
Egypt
'Ayn Umm al-Dabaqi: very well preserved early medieval mud-brick castle in a subsidiary oasis of the large Kharga oasis.

Before the American occupation of Iraq, the Iraqi government undertook a programme of restoration and, in too many cases, virtual reconstruction of the country's historical monuments. One site that received excessive attention was Qasr al-Ashiq, built for the caliph al-Mu'tamid between AD 878 and 882 on the eastern bank of the River Tigris, facing Samarra. (ABOVE LEFT) Qasr al-Ashiq as it was in the early 1970s. (ABOVE RIGHT) The fortified palace in the mid-1980s. (Author's photographs)

Tinnis: unexcavated ruins of an abandoned early Islamic port-city on an island in Lake Manzalah

Iran

Bam: ruins of early medieval citadel and walled city.

Bisatun: foundations and some ruins of a perhaps 10th-century fortified caravanserai.

Samiran: ruins of a medieval citadel.

Iraq

Atshan: ruins of what is probably a 7th-century fortified palace.

Kufa: excavated ruins of 7th–8th-century Dar al-Imara fortified governor's palace.

Samarra: ruins, foundations and several partial reconstructions of 9th–10th-century palaces, fortifications and many other buildings.

Ukhaidir: partially restored late 8th-century fortified palace.

Wasit: unexcavated ruins of 7th–8th-century Dar al-Imara fortified governor's palace and city walls.

Israel–Palestine

Acre: pre-Crusader structures including elements of fortification, especially beneath the Hospitaller citadel.

Arsuf: partially excavated urban fortifications.

Jericho (Khirbat al-Mafjir): excavated and partially restored ruins of early 8th-century so-called 'Hisham Palace'.

Jerusalem: excavated remains of Umayyad fortified palace complex next to the Haram al-Sharif 'Temple Mount'.

Kfar Lam: largely complete early Islamic coastal fort.

Jordan

Amman: fortifications and partially restored Umayyad palace complex on Jabal al-Qal'a.

Aqaba: excavated fortification of an early Islamic city.

Qasr al-Hallabat: Umayyad fortified 'desert palace'.

Qasr Harranah: Umayyad fortified 'desert palace'.

Qasr Burqu: Umayyad fortified 'desert palace'.

Qasr Tuba: Umayyad fortified 'desert palace'.

Mshatta: Umayyad fortified 'desert palace'.

Kyrghyzstan

Uzgend: 10th-century minaret and later mausoleums on what was one of the fortified hills of the early medieval Islamic frontier city.

Lebanon

Anjar: completely walled, partially excavated early 8th-century Umayyad fortified city.

Libya

Ajdabiyah: ruins of a 9th-century fortified palace.

Tocra: ruins of an Umayyad fort.

Madina Sultan: remains of fortified town and small separate fort.

Oman

Rustaq: early medieval Islamic triangular fortress, probably on pre-Islamic foundations.

Saudi Arabia

Rabadhah: excavated early Islamic pilgrimage way-station, including fortified structures.

Sud Samallaqi: early Islamic tower next to restored early medieval dam.

Suq Ukaz: early Islamic fortified market centre.

Ula: remains of early medieval Qal'ay Musa Ibn Nusair.

Syria

Damascus: National Museum, substantially reconstructed gate and decorated internal chambers of the 8th-century Umayyad 'desert palace' of Qasr al-Hayr al-Gharbi.

Kharab Sayar: ruins of early Islamic fortified town.

Qasr al-Hayr al-Gharbi: ruins of fortified Umayyad 8th-century 'desert palace'.

Qasr al-Hayr al-Sharqi: two fortified Umayyad 8th century enclosures, one in a remarkable state of repair.

Rahba: castle, the oldest parts of which date from the 11th century.

Raqqa: walls, gates and other buildings from the late 8th and 9th centuries.

Tajikistan

Mug-tepe: excavated pre- and early Islamic castle.

Ustrushana: excavated pre- and early Islamic town.

Turkey

Anazarva: ruins of early medieval citadel and urban fortifications.

Diyarbakr: virtually complete circuit wall, towers and gates of the old city.

Harran: 11th-century decorated gate.

Haruniye: substantially complete early Islamic castle.

Misis: unexcavated acropolis, site of early Islamic frontier fort.

Turkmenistan

Marw: substantial remains of multiple fortified enclosures from the early and later medieval periods.

Uzbekistan

Ribat-i-Malik: partial but still impressive remains of fortified caravanserai, perhaps partially dating from the early 11th century.

Kuva: excavated early medieval fortified town.

Shahrukhia: excavation of early Islamic fortified town.

BIBLIOGRAPHY

Abd al-Aziz, Sa'ad Bin, *Al-Rabadhah: Portrait of an Early Islamic Civilization in Saudi Arabia* (Riyadh, 1986).

Bahat, D., 'Les Portes de Jerusalem selon Mukaddasi, Nouvelle Identification', *Revue Biblique*, 93 (1986), 429–35.

Bakhit, M.A., and R. Schick (eds.), *The Fourth International Conference on the History of Bilad al-Sham During the Umayyad Period* (Amman, 1987), containing the following articles: Bisheh, G., 'Qasr Mshash and Qasr 'Ayn al-Sil: Two Umayyad Sites in Jordan', 81–103; Carlier, P., 'Qastal al-Balqa: An Umayyad Site in Jordan', 104–39; King, G.R.D., 'The Umayyad Qusur and Related Settlements in Jordan', 71–80.

Bell, G.L., *Ukhaidir* (Oxford, 1914).

Bentovich, I.B., 'Nakhodki na Gore Mug', *Materiali i Issledovaniya po Arckeologii SSSR*, 66 (1958), 358–83.

Bianquis, T., *Damas et la Syria sous la domination Fatimide (359-468/969-1076)* (Damascus, 1989).

Bosworth, C.E., 'Abu 'Amr 'Uthman al-Tarsusi's *Siyar al Thughur* and the Last Years of Arab Rule in Tarsus (Fourth/Tenth Century)', *Graeco-Arabica*, 5 (1993), 183–95.

Brun, P., and A. Annaev, 'The medieval fortifications', in G. Herrmann (et al. eds.), 'The International Merv Project, preliminary report of the ninth season (2000)', *Iran* (2001), 25–34.

Canard, M., 'Mutanabbi et la Guerre Byzantino-Arabe. Interet Historique de ses poesies', in (anon. ed.) *Al-Mutanabbi. Memoires de l'Institit Français de Damas* (Beirut, 1936), 100-110.

Christides, V., 'The Coastal Towns of Bilad al-Sham at the time of the Rashidun (632–661): Defence and Trade', *Epeteris tou Kentron Epistemonichon Ereunon*, 13–16 (1984–87), 49–62.

Creswell, K.A.C., 'Fortification in Islam before AD 1250', *Proceedings of the British Academy*, 38 (1952), 89–125 plus 16 plates.

Creswell, K.A.C., *The Muslim Architecture of Egypt* (reprint, New York, 1978).

Daiber, V. and A. Becker (eds.), *Raqqa III: Baudenkmaler und Palaste I* (Mainze, 2004).

Edwards, R.W., *The Fortifications of Armenian Cilicia* (Washington, 1987).

El'Ad, A., 'The Coastal Cities of Palestine during the Early Muslim Period', in L.I. Levine (ed.), *The Jerusalem Cathedra: Studies in the History, Archaeology, Geography and Ethnography of the Land of Israel, vol. II* (Jerusalem, 1982), 146–67.

El'Ad, A., 'The Siege of Wasit (132/749)', in M. Sharon (ed.), *Studies in Islamic History and Civilization in Honour of Professor David Ayalon* (Jerusalem, 1986), 59–90.

Finster, B., and J. Schmidt, *Sasanidische und Frühislamische Ruinen in Iraq (Baghdade Mitteilungen, vol. 8)* (Berlin, 1976).

Gabriel, A. 'Kasr el-Heir', *Syria*, 8 (1927), 302–29.

Gascoigne, A.L., 'An Archaeological Survey of Tell Tinnnis, Manzala, Egypt', *Antiquity*, 79 (March 2005).

Goiten, S.D., 'Jerusalem in the Arab Period (638–1099)', in L.I. Levine (ed.), *The Jerusalem Cathedra: Studies in the History, Archaeology, Geography and Ethnography of the Land of Israel, vol. II* (Jerusalem, 1982), 168–96.

Gough, M., 'Anarzarbus', *Anatolian Studies*, 2 (1952), 85–125.

Grabar, O. (et al.), *City in the Desert: Qasr al-Hayr East: Harvard Middle Eastern Monographs 23/24* (Cambridge, MA, 1978).

Hamilton, R.W., *Khirbat al-Mafjir* (Oxford, 1959).

Herzfeld, E., *Geschichte der Stadt Samarra* (Hamburg, 1948).

Innes MacAdam, H., 'Some Notes on the Umayyad Occupation of North-East Jordan', in P. Freeman and D. Kennnedy (eds.), *The Defence of the Roman and Byzantine East: BAR International Series, no. 297* (Oxford, 1986), 531–47.

Ivanov, G.P. (et al.), *Kubo City in Akhmad al-Fargoni's Epoch* (Tashkent, 1998).

Janabi, T. al-, 'Islamic Archaeology in Iraq: Recent Excavations at Samarra', *World Archaeology*, 14/3 (February 1983), 305–27.

Kennedy, H. (ed.), *Muslim Military Architecture in Greater Syria* (Leiden, 2006).

Kuhnel, E., *Mschatta: Bilderhefte der Islamischen Kunstabteilung, 2* (Berlin, 1933).

Kuhnel, E., *Samarra: Bilderhefte der Islamischen Kunstabteilung, 5* (Berlin, 1939).

Lammens, H., 'La cité arabe de Taif à la veille de l'Hegire', *Melanges de l'Université Saint-Joseph*, 8 (1922), 115–327.

Lassner, J., *The Topography of Baghdad in the Early Middle Ages* (Detroit, 1970).

Muaikel, K.I. al- (tr. G. El-Osman), 'Suq 'Ukaz in al-Ta'if: Archaeological Survey of an Islamic Site',

Al-'Usur al-Wusta: The Bulletin of Middle Eastern Medievalists, 7/1 (April 1995), 1–3, 16.

Mukhamedkhanov (et al. eds.), Gorodische Paikend (Tashkent, 1988).

Nasir-i Khusraw (G. Le Strange tr.), Diary of a Journey through Syria and Palestine by Nasir-i-Khusrau in 1047 AD (London, 1888); (G. Shefer tr.), Sefer Nameh: Relation du Voyage de Nassiri Khosrau (Paris, 1881).

Northedge, A., 'The Fortifications of Qal'at 'Amman ('Amman Citadel): Preliminary Report', Annual of the Department of Antiquity, 27 (1983), 437–59.

Reuther, O., Ocheidir (Leipzig, 1912).

Rice, D.S., 'Medieval Harran: Studies in its Topography and Monuments, I', Anatolian Studies, 2 (1952), 36–84.

Roll, I., 'Medieval Apollonia-Arsuf: A Fortified Coastal Town in the Levant of the Early Medieval and Crusader Periods', in M. Balard (ed.), Autour de la Première Croisade (Paris, 1996), 595–606.

Safar, Fuad, Wasit, the Sixth Season's Excavations (Cairo, 1945).

Sauvaget, J., 'Les Ruines omeyyades de 'Andjarr', Bulletin de Musee de Beyrouth, 3 (1939).

Stern, H., 'Notes sur l'architecture des Chateaux Omeyyades', Ars Islamica, 11–12 (1946), 87–93.

Wormhoudt, A. (tr.), Dhikra Saif al Daula (Pennsylvania, 1975).

The existing urban defences of the south-eastern Turkish city of Diyarbakr fall into two distinct categories. The early medieval Islamic southern walls have polygonal towers with smaller rectangular towers in between; those seen here are near the Mardin Kapasi, 'Mardin Gate', where there were no suburbs in the 1970s. (Author's photograph)

The standard of construction in the so-called Umayyad 'desert palaces' in the steppe regions of Syria and Jordan, varied a great deal. One of the finest, in terms of masonry and carved decoration, is at Mshatta. (Author's photograph)

GLOSSARY

ajurr   baked brick, fired brick (Arabic).

ambar, anbar   military store or arsenal on a frontier of the Sassanian Empire (Farsi).

ark   citadel (Farsi).

'awasim   defensive provinces immediately to rear of *thughur* military frontier provinces (Arabic).

bab   gate (Arabic).

bashura   change of angle in the entrance path or corridor within a 'bent entrance' gate complex (Arabic).

bayt   system of organizing the internal rooms of a building into separate, self-contained units (literally 'house', Arabic).

birun   outer town or suburb (Farsi).

burj   tower (Arabic).

dar al-imara   government headquarters, usually provincial or regional and often fortified (Arabic).

dihliz   covered hallway, vestibule or chamber forming part of a gate or fortified complex (Farsi).

dimas   dungeon or unlit vault (Arabic).

diwan   government ministry in which official business was conducted (Arabic).

diz   fortress or fortified city (Farsi).

fasil   area enclosed by a low wall ahead of the main defences (Arabic).

firdaws   enclosed garden, usually palatial (Farsi).

hamam   bath complex (Arabic).

hayr   large enclosed space, often as game reserve for hunting (Arabic).

hisn   specifically military and fortified structure (Arabic).

hubus   prison (Arabic).

ikhata   process of outlining the foundations of a building before construction (Arabic).

iwan   tall vaulted chamber, usually open at one end (Arabic and Farsi).

jisr   bridge (Arabic).

kala   castle (Turkish, from Arabic *qal'a*).

khandaq   ditch or moat (Arabic).

khanqah   'convent', sometimes referring to barracks for religiously motivated volunteers (Arabic).

kuhandiz   citadel (Farsi).

madina   main part of a town or city (Arabic).

manazir   watchtowers (Arabic).

markaz   way-stations for the *barid* government postal service (Arabic).

maydan   open area for military parades and cavalry training (Arabic).

mintar   watchtower (Arabic).

misr   garrison settlement or cantonment (Arabic).

mizallah   shelter, often to protect horses from the sun (Arabic).

pakhsa   large building blocks made of earth and straw (Turkish).

qal'a   castle – though this meaning was not universal in the very early Islamic period (Arabic).

qasr   high-status building, but not necessarily fortified (Arabic).

qubbah   dome or domed building or structure (Arabic).

rabid   outer town or suburb, originally meaning area where animals were gathered (Arabic).

ribat   frontier or coastal location garrisoned for defence.

rukn   supports, prop or corner of a fortified structure (Arabic).

rustaq   district or unspecific 'lands', or rural or oasis area surrounding a landholder's castle (Farsi).

sadd   barrier, usually a dam, but also a fortified 'long wall' (Farsi from Arabic *sudd*).

shadakhat   cross-beams or boards with protruding spikes forming a defensive feature (literally 'crushers', Arabic).

shahristan   central town of a *shahr* district, usually fortified, or the main part of a town or city, usually fortified (Farsi).

shaqif   cave-refuge (Arabic).

shurafat   battlements (Arabic).

sur   fortified circuit wall of a town or other enclosed area (Arabic).

sitr   protective screen (Arabic).

tarimah   balcony, kiosk, part of a citadel where a ruler showed himself to the people (Arabic).

tawb   unbaked brick, mud brick (Arabic).

thughur   frontier provinces under military administration (Arabic).

utum   tower as a place of refuge (Arabic).

zardkhanah   weapons store (Arabic and Farsi).

zawiyah   'house of spiritual refuge', sometimes referring to barracks for religiously motivated volunteers (Arabic).

INDEX